Find Your GROOVE

A guide to discovering your scrapbook style

Kitty Foster and Wendy McKeehan

Memory Makers Books
Cincinnati, Ohio
www.memorymakersmagazine.com

About the Authors

Kitty Foster has been writing, designing and teaching in the scrapbooking field since the year 2000. She has been published in many major scrapbooking magazines and idea books throughout the years. She has taught at scrapbooking retreats, conventions and even on a scrapbook cruise in January 2005. Kitty also is part of design teams for several manufacturers. When not scrapbooking, you can often find her taking photographs on the sideline of one of her kid's sporting events, wearing funky jeans or reading the obituaries.

Wendy McKeehan has been involved in the scrapbooking industry since its infancy. She has done everything from demonstrating to teaching to layout design to product testing to consulting to writing articles and getting a few pages of her own done here and there. Wendy is a member of a manufacturer design team and is former Contributing Editor for DesignerZine.com. When she's not scrapping the moment you will find her singing in the church choir, attending her kids' events or kicking back with a glass of red wine.

Find Your Groove. Copyright © 2007 by Kitty Foster and Wendy McKeehan. Manufactured in Singapore. All rights reserved. It is permissible for the purchaser to make the projects contained herein and sell them at fairs, bazaars and craft shows. No other part of this book may be reproduced in any form or by any electronic or mechanical means including information storage and retrieval systems without permission in writing from the publisher, except by a reviewer, who may quote a brief passage in review. Published by Memory Makers Books, an imprint of F+W Publications, Inc., 4700 East Galbraith Road, Cincinnati, Ohio 45236. (800) 289-0963. First edition.

11 10 09 08 07   5 4 3 2 1

Distributed in Canada by Fraser Direct
100 Armstrong Avenue
Georgetown, ON, Canada L7G 5S4
Tel: (905) 877-4411

Distributed in the U.K. and Europe by David & Charles
Brunel House, Newton Abbot, Devon, TQ12 4PU, England
Tel: (+44) 1626 323200, Fax: (+44) 1626 323319
E-mail: postmaster@davidandcharles.co.uk

Distributed in Australia by Capricorn Link
P.O. Box 704, S. Windsor, NSW 2756 Australia
Tel: (02) 4577-3555

Editor: Christine Doyle
Designer: Marissa Bowers
Layout Artist: Kelly O'Dell
Illustrations: Kristi Smith and Aruna Rangarajan,
                Anderson Thomas Design, Inc.
Art Coordinator: Eileen Aber
Production Coordinator: Matthew Wagner
Photographer: Christine Polomsky

Digital brushes courtesy of Katie Pertiet and
Anna Aspnes of designerdigitals.com.

Library of Congress Cataloging-in-Publication Data
Foster, Kitty
  Find your groove : a guide to discovering your scrapbook style / Kitty
Foster and Wendy McKeehan.
    p. cm.
  Includes index.
  ISBN-13: 978-1-59963-006-9 (alk. paper)
  ISBN-10: 1-59963-006-0 (alk. paper)
  1. Photograph albums. 2. Photographs--Conservation and restoration. 3.
Scrapbooks. I. McKeehan, Wendy II. Title.
  TR465.F52 2007
  745.593--dc22

                                2007006740

We dedicate this book to:

My God—thank you for all the blessings you have given and your constant patience and love for me. To my husband of 19 years who put up with my late nights and dusty furniture during crunch time and to our four kids who were patient with me even when I had the camera in their faces. Thank you to my parents who not only raised me in the faith but made me feel that I could do anything, to my sister Penny who is my best friend for life, and to my friends who believed in me and encouraged me to take this big leap of faith. To my church, Grace Fellowship—thank you for giving me a place to refuel each Sunday. Many thanks to my high school and college English teachers who will sit in shock when they find out that their mediocre student who butchered the English language on a daily basis has written a book. I'm just as surprised as you are!

Kitty

My husband Chris, who totally "gets" this scrapbooking phenomenon and forgives my inept housecleaning skills while I follow my dreams. Oh wait, I have always had inept housecleaning skills. To Connor, Tori and Zoë who are my reason, my inspiration and my pure joy. To Mom and Dad for always being proud of my successes, regardless of my age. To my sister Nikki, who's creative footsteps I hope to one day fill. And finally, to my scrapping sisters—the best thing this hobby/passion/obsession has brought me is the friendship I share with you all. Thank you.

Wen

Acknowledgments

Much gratitude to these companies for their sponsorship of this book: American Crafts, Cosmo Cricket, A2Z Essentials, SugarLoaf Products, Krylon, Mustard Moon, Making Memories, Therm O Web, Worldwin Cardstock, Cherry Arte, Junkitz, Creative Imaginations, Karen Foster, My Minds Eye, Maya Road, Scenic Route and Imagination Project.

Many thanks to Christine Doyle who believed in two silly girls with a dream. We thank for your encouragement, guidance and for laughing at our jokes.

Special appreciation to our unofficial and unpaid consultants, Kitty's friend Shannan Browning and Wendy's sister Nikki Shannon.

Thank you to the wonderful contributors who helped make the book what it is: Audrey Neal, Karen Burniston, Cheryl Manz, Helen McCain, Kathleen Summers, Kelly Goree, Mindy Bush, Shannon Landen, Stephanie Vetne, Deena Wuest, Alexis Hardy, Kathe Cunningham, Janet Ohlsen, Alecia Grimm, Kathleen Paneitz, Sharyn Tormanen, Vicki Harvey and Kimber McGray.

To the incredible artists that are in the gallery: thank you for believing in us enough to contribute. Your work made this book complete!

Thanks Al!

Every presidential campaign has many snafus, but the one that has always stood out to me is from Al Gore. Many funny statements were made during the 2000 campaign from both opponents, but my favorite is when my boy Al said he invented the internet. Of course he didn't and that was what made it all the more entertaining. In a funny way, this brings me to Wendy. A few years ago, Wendy and I were working on a project for a company along with many other scrapbookers. I was the only name on the list that she recognized (so she says) and she contacted me with questions about our project. We instantly connected and laughed about our shared confusion and an online friendship was born. We were later blessed to be able to meet in person and in time our friendship has developed deeper. So I guess one could say that if it wasn't for the internet, Wendy and I would have never met – thanks Al!

August, 2006

August 2006 - Destin, FL

Lucy and Ethel, Thelma and Louise, Oprah and Gayle, they've got nothin' on Kitty and Wendy. A chance meeting at a trade show after "knowing" each other on the message boards was all it took. Now we've traveled the country together, written a book and laughed more than should be allowed by law. It's been a great ride...so far!

It's a Groove Thing

Madonna sang about it in the '80s.
Stella got hers back in the '90s.
Then the Emperor got a new one.

What are we talking about?

We are talking about groove.

Can you hear Austin Powers in your head? "Groovy baby yeah!" We're not talking about the grooves in your old records, we're talking about:

groove n. : A situation or activity to which one is especially well suited; niche.

When it comes to your scrapbook pages, have you ever asked the question, "What is my style?" Have you ever wondered how to go about finding it? And once you find it, have you ever wondered how to keep it going? Have you ever found yourself in a creative rut and wondered if there were some steps to get out of it? If you have ever asked those questions, then come along with us as we quiz, question, examine, challenge and reveal your scrapbooking niche!

The search

So what are you looking for? Design tips? A cohesive style? A renewed excitement about your style and your art? Then you have picked up the right book.

Every time you start something new in your life, the same process has to happen. Life can get a little chaotic until you get a routine or find your rhythm. Whether it is a new job, a recent move or even a vacation, it is always the same. It all starts to work together harmoniously once you discover the ebb and flow. Scrapbooking is no different. Once your creativity starts to flow, you will find your groove and your pages come together almost effortlessly. Less effort and good design—doesn't that sound like a dream come true?

It's all about you

As you take this journey, you will discover many things about yourself and that includes your design DNA. Just as the little twisty ties in your cells are a road map to who you are as a person, your design DNA is as individual as you are and no two people are exactly alike. In this book we will discover what makes your style unique and personal to you—that special something that makes your art distinctly yours. It is a fun process that is worth your time. So grab your favorite beverage, a pen and make an appointment with yourself to begin the steps of discovering your scrapbook style.

EVERY PAGE YOU *create* REFLECTS WHO YOU *are.*

Chapter 1

What's Your Style?

When asked how they would describe their artistic style, most scrapbookers tend to get a puzzled look in their eye. The reason for this may simply be that they have never taken the time to explore the various styles out there and determine what it is that appeals to them visually and emotionally. That is where this book comes in! We are here to take you on the journey toward "style self-discovery." There are a few steps that will help you figure out what your unique design DNA is. Let's jump in!

style (n.) An artist's characteristic manner of expression

We all know artists that have distinctive styles. These are artists whose artwork is very recognizable. Picasso had his cubistic works, Monet led the impressionist movement, and Ansel Adams almost always photographed natural subjects in black and white. You may even have a few favorite scrapbook artists whose pages you always recognize. It could be the creative way they use patterned paper, their whimsical product usage or their amazing photography, but they seem to have something consistent that they do on every page that is unique to them.

In this book, we're on the hunt for your "characteristic manner of expression"—your special design "something." We like to think that everyone has their own specific scrapbook DNA. No two scrapbookers are exactly alike, and therefore, no two styles will be exactly alike either. Your artform is fiercely tied to your personal emotions, loved ones and passions, so every page you create reflects who you are.

Just as every exercise routine starts with a good warm up, we're going to get you ready to think about your personal style with a warm up exercise.

Let's start by taking a short quiz to get you thinking specifically about how you design your pages.

everyone has their own specific SCRAPBOOK DNA

When it comes to paper or backgrounds

(select one or two):

- [ ] I'll stick to cardstock, thank you very much. **(1)**
- [ ] I love a classic plaid, stripe or polka dot— just not for bikinis. **(4)**
- [ ] I like patterns as long as they color coordinate. I'm high maintenance that way. **(4)**
- [ ] I am all about the art and like to use everything. Color wheels are for chumps! **(8)**
- [ ] I love the hip and cool geometric patterns inspired by the 60's. Make scrapbooks not war. **(7)**
- [ ] I get inspiration from clothing catalogs and fabrics. Isn't that what they are for? **(7)**
- [ ] I'll take any paper as long as I can distress it! **(5)**
- [ ] I favor graphic papers. Bold patterns and color combos draw me in. **(2)**
- [ ] I love vintage prints…toile is dreamy! **(6)**
- [ ] A soft subtle floral make me swoon. **(5)**
- [ ] Papers you choose go with the mood you want for the page. In my albums, one page will have soft colors and the other bold. **(3)**

When it comes to embellishments and extras

(select one or two):

- [ ] Yo Yo! It's all about the bling baby! **(7)**
- [ ] Vintage buttons, ribbons and lace put a smile on my face! **(6)**
- [ ] I never met a chipboard I didn't like. **(3)**
- [ ] Bring on the funky stuff…ghost shapes, transparencies, paint pens, office supplies, you name it! **(8)**
- [ ] I rarely use embellishments…guess I should stop buying them! **(1)**
- [ ] I love to use accents that coordinate with papers to create a cohesive look. **(4)**
- [ ] Accents are just that…accents; they should not take focus away from the photos. **(2)**
- [ ] I love to use found objects in surprising ways on my pages. **(8)**
- [ ] I like to embrace my inner white space. **(1)**

- [ ] I love to use the latest and greatest! I am first in line at the local scrapbook store when the new products arrive. I even help them unpack. **(7)**
- [ ] Like brown paper packages tied up with string, distress inks and sanding blocks are a few of my favorite things! **(5)**
- [ ] I don't use a lot of embellishments, but I love to use a few to break up the lines on the page and add visual flow. **(3)**

When it comes to page design (select only one):

- [ ] I love a clean look to my pages… squares are my friend. **(1)**
- [ ] My pages are rarely square. There's usually something hanging off the side or a decorative treatment done to the edge. Nothing is sacred! **(8)**
- [ ] I prefer straight lines, coordinated products and two-page spreads. **(4)**
- [ ] I just can't seem to leave a page alone…it's got to be inked, painted, crumpled, sanded or sewn to be complete. **(5)**
- [ ] The body of the layout may have a clean lined look until the final curved element is added over top. There has to be a little playfulness about the page. **(3)**
- [ ] I've been known to sketch advertisements from magazines and even building shapes. Pitiful, aren't I? **(7)**
- [ ] I have been known to measure the margins on my page to make sure they are equal…it's a sickness, I know. **(1)**
- [ ] I'm always trying to push the envelope on my pages, so they rarely look alike. I'm all over the map! **(3)**
- [ ] I always plan the page carefully, intending to draw the eye to the focal point. **(2)**
- [ ] When I'm done, I hope the page is soft and warm. Just like my favorite old quilt. **(6)**

When it comes to photos on my pages

(select only one):

- [ ] I tend to prefer one-photo pages. **(1)**
- [ ] I love using lots of pics on my pages in all kinds of fun sizes from index prints to 10" x 10" (25cm x 25cm). **(3)**
- [ ] No fear…I journal on photos, tear them, paint on them, staple them. You name it, I've tried it. **(8)**

- [ ] I like to use digital filters on my photos for unique looks like graphite pencil, watercolor and mosaic. **(7)**
- [ ] I love the look of sepia tone and hand-tinted photos. **(6)**
- [ ] I like to mat my photos. **(4)**
- [ ] I rarely print anything other than 4" x 6" (10cm x 15cm). **(4)**
- [ ] I love enlargements on a page. **(2)**
- [ ] Every once and awhile I use an oddly shaped or circular photo. **(3)**
- [ ] I enjoy distressing the edges of my photos or printing them out on canvas for a softer look. **(5)**

In regard to type on my pages (select only one):

- [ ] An eye-catching title grabs my attention every time. **(2)**
- [ ] I like to pull my titles out of my journaling. The journaling and the title flow together. **(3)**
- [ ] Takes me forever to find the perfect font for my page….it's like a scavenger hunt! **(1)**
- [ ] I like to hand write my journaling on pages because I feel that my handwriting is part of my legacy. **(4)**
- [ ] Those old-fashioned script fonts always catch my eye. **(6)**
- [ ] Fonts are not a big deal for me. I use them for journaling, but I stick with a few favorites. **(4)**
- [ ] I'm all about mixing it up. Some fonts, some handwriting, some doodling—it's all good. **(8)**
- [ ] I enjoy using different fonts and getting a whimsical look with my titles or journaling. **(3)**
- [ ] The fonts that are a bit beat up are my faves: old typewriter, hand stamped alphas and worn typefaces. **(5)**
- [ ] I am a font junkie! I add at least two new fonts a month to my collection! **(7)**

When it comes to color (select one or two):

- [ ] I am always inspired by the latest colors in fashion. Move over Oscar de la Renta! **(7)**
- [ ] I love soft subtle colors—pastels or neutrals. **(5)**
- [ ] Colors are used to show the emotion of the page— to capture what I want to document. **(3)**
- [ ] I love vibrant colors. The page has to *pop*! **(3)**
- [ ] I pick colors to grab the eye. They aren't necessarily bright, just eye catching. **(2)**
- [ ] A variety of color schemes can be used in one layout. It is more about artful expression than anything. **(8)**
- [ ] I love to use black and white for drama. **(1)**
- [ ] I'm matchy matchy—colors need to match up. Long live color wheels! **(4)**
- [ ] A lot of my pages start with a white background. **(1)**
- [ ] I think the colors of the Scooby Doo mystery machine are groovy, baby! **(7)**
- [ ] The grungier the better. **(5)**
- [ ] Primary colors totally make a page. **(4)**
- [ ] I'm drawn to the deep rich color schemes. I shy away from the really bright colors. **(6)**

Tally up the points from each question to start getting an idea of your personal style

0–15	Clean lines
15–25	Graphic
26–35	Eclectic
36–40	Classic
40–51	Shabby or Old World
52–63	Hip and Trendy
64+	Anything Goes

These categories represent eight primary styles of scrapbook pages that we'll refer to throughout the book. (The ninth style we cover is journalistic. But because the actual look of the pages vary from shabby to graphic, it is not included in the quiz.) You may not completely agree with our definitions, and that is fine. Style is not so precise that it has to fit in one box and one box alone.

Note, too, that you can certainly straddle the lines of styles. Any of these categories can be put together to create a whole new look. Heck, Kitty considers herself to be Shabby Neat; she fits somewhere between Shabby and Clean Lines. But without the definitions to start with, Kitty could not define her own style.

We've asked our crack team of scrapbook designers to use the same photos of Kitty's daughter, Hannah, to illustrate each style. Following are those layouts and definitions of each style to help you start to figure out where your style fits in.

Hannah, you are becoming quite the young woman and less a little girl every day. Remember, though that life isn't about rushing to be a grown-up. There's still plenty of time to dance... love, Mom

Clean Lines

A cleanly designed page does not necessarily mean simply designed. The edges of the photos as well as the page tend to be clearly defined. Layouts in this category will work around a grid and be very neat. The designs follow a predictable pattern and are therefore calming to the eye. This style leads the eye to the photos on the page in an organized way and has a striking look to it that is crisp and clean.

Kathe Cunningham, Buford, Georgia

Supplies: Cardstock (Bazzill); patterned paper (K&Co.); ribbons (Offray, Textured Trios); flowers (Heidi Swapp); acrylic paint, rhinestone brads (Making Memories); chipboard corner (Deluxe Designs); chalk ink (Clearsnap); pen; zip dry adhesive (Beacon); Murray Bold font (Internet download)

Hannah,

You are becoming quite the young woman and less a little girl every day. Remember, though that life isn't about rushing to be a grown-up. There's still plenty of time to dance.

Love, Mom

forever young

HANNAH

「Graphic」

This page style jumps out and grabs you. It says, "Look at me!" Pages done in this style are visually stunning and tend to surprise you with their design. They tend to be random in their pattern and can use interesting angles. Where a clean-lined page tends to follow a grid, the graphic pages usually draw your eye to the focal point using a broken grid. These designs are more subjective and usually have a great energy about them.

Linda Harrison, Sarasota, Florida

Supplies: Cardstock (Bazzill); chipboard letters and accents (Heidi Swapp); clip, flower (Doodlebug); ribbon (SEI); chalk ink (Clearsnap); Sans Serif font (Microsoft)

For Hannah
Love Mom

You are becoming
quite the young woman
and less a little girl every day.
Remember, though, that life isn't
about rushing to be a grown
up. There's still plenty
of time to

Eclectic

Many people would probably describe themselves as eclectic in their scrapbooking style. They aren't beholden to one design style or another, but tend to mix it up a bit. The body of the layout may have a clean-lined look until the final curved element is added over top. An Old World Charm layout may be updated a bit with vibrant colors or shapes. This is a broad style that is very flexible. It tends to be whimsical and playful in nature.

Kathleen Paneitz, Loveland, Colorado

Supplies: Cardstock; patterned paper (Making Memories, MOD); letter stickers (K&Co.); rub-on letters, tag (Making Memories); chipboard flowers (Imagination Project); decorative tape (Heidi Swapp); brads (Bazzill); ribbon (Offray); circle cutter; pen; zip dry adhesive (Beacon); Blissful font (Two Peas in a Bucket)

Classic

A classic page is one with great bones. The layout of the page is strong and unassuming. The eye goes directly to the photos and follows them through the page. Typically the photos on these pages are 4" x 6" (10cm x 15cm) or 3" x 5" (8cm x 13cm), with an occasional enlargement, and there are multiple photos on a page. Techniques are rarely used and accents are used as they were intended. Two-page spreads are common and journaling is always visible. These pages tend to be safe and traditional in their design and use coordinated kits or product lines to get a cohesive look. Patterned papers are often used in small amounts. Patterns don't have to match but colors need to be compatible.

Sharyn Tormanen, Howell, Michigan

Supplies: Patterned paper (Dèjá Views, Die Cuts With A View); scalloped cardstock (Bazzill); letter stamps (Technique Tuesday); flowers (Doodlebug, Heidi Swapp); brad; chalk ink (Tsukineko); Garamond font (Microsoft)

Hannah,

You are becoming quite the young woman
and less a little girl every day.
Remember, though that life isn't about
rushing to be a grown-up. There's still
plenty of time to dance!

Love,
Mom

Old World Charm

Also known as Vintage or Romantic, this style harkens back to yesteryear.
Black and white photos, lace, vintage fabrics and notions are often used on
these pages. It also lends itself to antiquing of elements with walnut inks,
paints, tea staining and watercolors. Old World Charm often has soft colors
with a subtle sense of pattern. Just like the name sounds, it combines the
look of the old country with a vintage charm.

Katie Pertiet, Ellicott City, Maryland

Supplies: Digital paper, binder slide, deckled frame, fasteners, letters, tags (Designer Digitals);
AL Cadence font (Autumn Leaves)

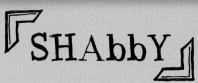

〚SHAbbY〛

Shabby styles often use dainty English florals or stripes and can have the charm of a damask napkin or the warmth of an old quilt. It has a distressed elegance that gives a feeling of age with a certain charm. There is also a cleaner look that isn't quite so distressed but still has softened edges and rounded corners. Both looks are soft and blend the photos, journaling and embellishments into a seamless page. The shabby look often appears grungy and uses elements such as torn paper, inked edges, rolled paper, random sewing and distressed papers.

Vicki Harvey, Champlin, Minnesota

Supplies: Patterned paper (Making Memories, Melissa Frances, Mustard Moon); rub-on letters (Mustard Moon); tag (Avery); buttons, lace (unknown); flowers, ribbon (Michaels); photo corners (Canson); decorative scissors; thread; pen; Scrapbook font (Two Peas in a Bucket)

Hip and Trendy

There are always trends and people willing to follow them in the world of design. These pages are cutting edge and new. They capture the hottest looks in fashion, home décor and advertising. The layouts that fit this category use one or several of the latest trends to make the page come to life. These designs are where it's at.

Alexis Hardy, Franklin Square, New York

Supplies: Cardstock (Bazzill); patterned paper (Hambly, Scenic Route, Urban Lily); letter stickers (American Crafts); chipboard accents (Heidi Swapp, Imagination Project, Urban Lily); circle stamp (Technique Tuesday); dye ink; rub-on accents (Urban Lily); buttons, photo corners (unknown); dimensional paint; pen

dance

HANNAH

you're becoming quite the young woman and less a little girl every day.

Remember, though, that life isn't about rushing to be a grownup. There's still plenty of time to dance.

love,
Mom ♥

⌜Anything Goes⌟

Some artists can look at a variety of supplies (scrapbook or otherwise) and create amazing art combinations. Artists who are comfortable with this style can make art out of anything and everything. They show their creativity by combining unusual products together to make one artful piece. As the name suggests, any and all products can be used to create this look. The talent is knowing when to say when—just like at a good buffet! This style often lends itself more toward art than documenting memories. It is designing according to whim rather than a prescribed style. This can be very freeing and liberating.

Janet Ohlson, Plainfield, Illinois

Supplies: Cardstock (Bazzill); patterned paper (7 Gypsies, American Crafts, Arctic Frog, BasicGrey, Hambly, Making Memories, Paper Source, Scenic Route); chipboard letters (Scenic Route); stamp accents (Stamped In Ink, Sugarloaf); dye ink (Tsukineko); circle sticker (Chatterbox); beads (Michaels); jewel accents (Heidi Swapp); metal flowers (Creative Imagination); sticker accents (Making Memories); glitter; pen

Hannah girl,

The Bible tells us that for everything there is a season and here we are in a different season of life with you—The beginning of High School. Recently, I started thinking about things differently. Instead of thinking that we only have you at home for 4 more years, I thought about this time in seasons. There are only 4 more winters, 4 more springs, 4 more summers and 4 more falls that you will be with us. How will we make the most of them? What memories will we make? Some will be big, but most will be small like this one.

girly
twirly

On this summer day, you were just being the girl that you are and I love that. Ever since you were little, you always checked every skirt for what you called the "twirl factor." How much a skirt could spin determined how much you liked it (& wore it!) Today was no different there you are, all 14 years of you and you still enjoy twirling around in a skirt. That's my girl! It has been both a joy and a privilege to have you as a daughter. A daughter is such a great responsibility, one that I do not take lightly.

Thank you!
Love, Mom

⌜Journalistic⌟

These pages can be in any of the previous eight styles but are also journaling focused. The products used and the designs made are more simplistic so that the focus is on the photos and journaling. The journaling is usually visible on these pages and used as one of the focal points of the design. Whether from the funny bone or the heart, the journaling is where the structure begins. The goal here is to create a visual story with the words. The photos and embellishments on the page are the icing on the cake.

Kimber McGray, Carmel, Indiana

Supplies: Cardstock; patterned paper (Scrapworks, We R Memory Keepers); plastic letters (Heidi Swapp); chipboard accent (We R Memory Keepers); corner rounder; embroidery floss; dye ink (Ranger); sandpaper; pen

NO MAN HAS THE RIGHT TO
DICTATE WHAT OTHER MEN
SHOULD PERCEIVE, CREATE
OR PRODUCE, BUT ALL SHOULD
BE ENCOURAGED TO REVEAL
THEMSELVES, THEIR PERCEPT-
IONS AND EMOTIONS, AND
TO BUILD CONFIDENCE IN THE
CREATIVE SPIRIT.

Ansel Adams

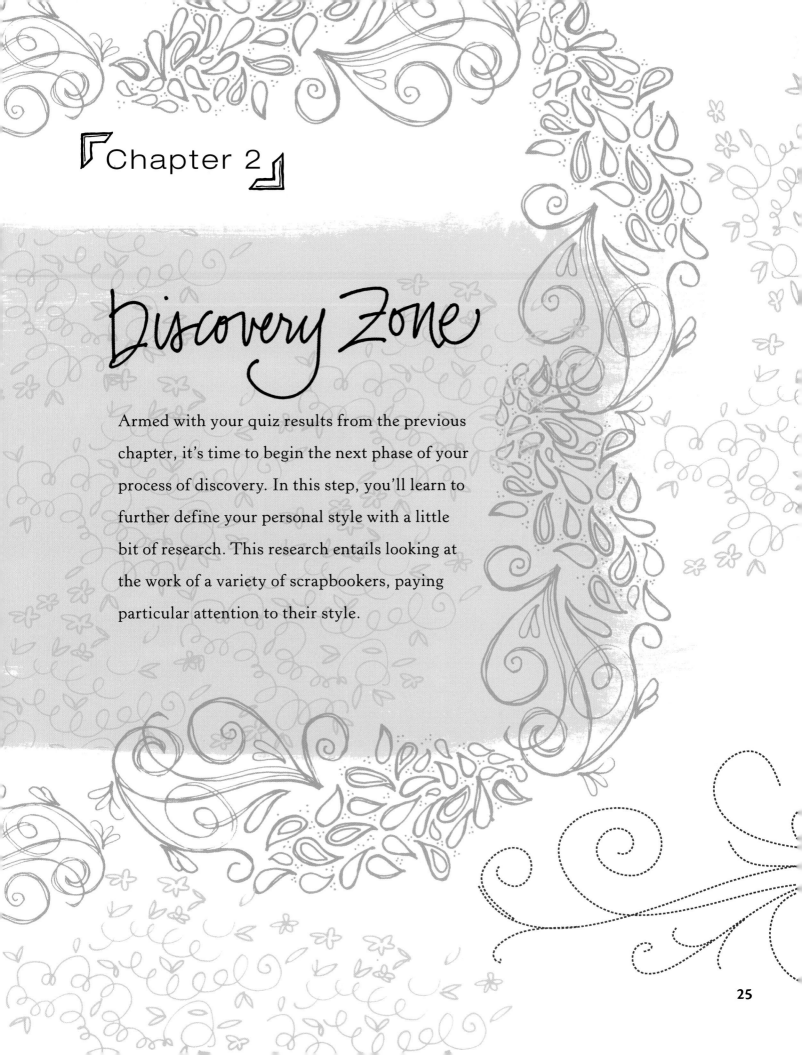

Chapter 2

Discovery Zone

Armed with your quiz results from the previous chapter, it's time to begin the next phase of your process of discovery. In this step, you'll learn to further define your personal style with a little bit of research. This research entails looking at the work of a variety of scrapbookers, paying particular attention to their style.

If a layout stands out to you, it does so for a reason—whether it is color choices, picture placement or overall design. You can browse books, magazines, online galleries and see what designs catch your eye.

When you start browsing, keep an open mind and don't limit your searches by product lines or media (digital vs. paper). Try not to think about colors you have in mind for a particular project or any supplies you have on hand. You want to look at each style with a fresh perspective—to look at it as if for the first time. See the layout as a whole instead of just individual elements on a page. If the page brings a smile to your face, mark it.

Finding designs that consistently draw your eye will take a little time, but it's well worth the effort. It's like shopping for that great pair of jeans. We usually have to try on at least ten pair to find the ones that are the right fit, and it's the same way with discovering your style.

As you continue your journey, look at a lot of pages and make a few notes along the way. You will start to see what really appeals to you as well as what styles don't. This helps you to narrow in on your overall focus. You will probably find a variety of styles that you are drawn to, but try to focus on one or two styles at a time for clarity.

To get you started on the path toward style enlightenment, here are a few pages that represent the styles listed in chapter one. Take a minute to see which ones immediately catch your eye and if you can figure out which category (or categories) they fall into. The style of each layout is identified on page 35.

Developing a personal style is not copying someone else's style.

Back(pack) 2 School
Kelly Goree, Shelbyville, Kentucky

Supplies: Cardstock (WorldWin); patterned paper (Adorn It, BasicGrey, Karen Foster); chipboard letters (BasicGrey, CherryArte); chipboard circle (CherryArte); ribbon (Making Memories); rub-on accents (Karen Foster); die-cut tags (Sizzix); embroidery floss; acrylic paint (Plaid); paperclip; pigment ink (Clearsnap); pen; tape runner adhesive (Therm O Web)

see for yourself

Prague is such a beautiful city. It has such an old-world feel, almost as though you are stepping back in time. The architecture is incredible - There's so much to see.

travel

escape.

destination

Prague
Audrey Neal
Clinton, Kentucky

Supplies: Patterned paper, chipboard accents (Scenic Route); acrylic paint (Making Memories); brads; cardboard; envelope; grid paper; pigment ink (Clearsnap, Stampin' Up); stamps (Sugarloaf); pen; zip dry adhesive (Beacon)

Wishing For Rainbows
Cheryl Manz, Deerfield, Illinois

Supplies: Patterned paper (American Crafts, KI Memories, Scenic Route); transparency (Hambly); black letter stickers (American Crafts); red letter stickers (unknown); flowers (Heidi Swapp); brads; chipboard accent (Scenic Route); marker

WISHING FOR RAINBOWS

julia: cheryl we want to tell you what we wish for when we throw pennies in the wishing fountain.

me: you can't tell me... wishes have to be secret or they don't come true."

eric: but we NEED to tell you... it's important."

me: ok, what do you wish for?"

julia: we wish for "Rainbows!"

me: what a GREAT wish! I LOVE Rainbows!"

eric + julia: we already know that... that's why we always wish for them.

unforgettable.

The Madison Wisconsin Capitol Building

capitol

E L P O S A L E

2 3 4 5 6 7 8 9 0

Walking around the city of Madison with Erin's Girl Scout troop, before the ballet at the Overture theatre, we visited Capitol Square hoping to visit inside. It was closed, but made a great photo.

December, 2004

Capitol
Helen McCain
Sun Prairie, Wisconsin

Supplies: Patterned paper (Creative Imaginations, My Mind's Eye); patterned transparency, rub-on accents (My Mind's Eye); fabric flower (Making Memories); paper flowers (Prima); rhinestones (K&Co.); rickrack (BasicGrey); hinge (Daisy D's); fabric (unknown); transparency (Grafix); vellum runner, zots adhesive (Therm O Web)

The Kaleidoscope of My Life
Wendy McKeehan
Batavia, Illinois

Supplies: Patterned paper (BasicGrey); letter stickers (Mustard Moon); rub-on letters (7 Gypsies); rectangle punch; canvas (Creative Imaginations); chalk ink (Craf-T); tape runner adhesive (3L)

HOPE KINDNESS SEARCHING JOY GRACE
ANGER REGRETS FRIENDSHIP
DREAMS TEARS
PRAYER DARING GRIEF
PROMISES PEACE
LOVE WONDERMENT
CHAOS MEMORIES RISKS PATHWAYS
THE KALEIDOSCOPE OF AWE FAITH
FEAR SOLITUDE LOSS
MY Life

Ouch
Kathleen Summers
Roseville, California

Supplies: Cardstock (WorldWin); patterned paper (Chatterbox, Junkitz, Making Memories); letter stamps (Sugarloaf); acrylic paint; chipboard accents (Junkitz); rub-on accents (7 Gypsies); sticker border (Making Memories); flower brads (Creative Imaginations); twill (Autumn Leaves); buttons; dye ink (Ranger); sandpaper; pen; adhesive (Therm O Web)

a fall, a trip to the ER, a rough day

We were in San Ramon after signing the loan docs, having coffee at Starbuck's with Rob & Clelia. The kids were playing outside up on the top of a concrete planter. Ron and I didn't see it happen, but Rob saw it and said "Holly fell" and we all went running outside. Her shoelace had caught on a bush and she fell face first down to the concrete ground. We could see that the gash at the top of her forehead was pretty deep and that she'd need stitches so we went to the ER. It was nice that her Tia & Tio and even grandma were there . . . . but it was. . . . well, it was just one of those days.

E- You have always loved the Splash Pool at Clear Creek. This year though, I'm betting you rethought that opinion with the water being so icy cold! 6/2006

and outta control!

TOUGHEN UP

Wet & Wild
Kelly Goree
Shelbyville, Kentucky

Supplies: Cardstock (Bazzill); patterned paper, chipboard letters, plastic letters, rub-on accents (Heidi Swapp); chipboard circle (WorldWin); pen; tape runner adhesive (Therm O Web)

PiercedEars

GOOD TIMES

just got my ears pierced at claire's

PARTY TIP No 1.9 J LIFE IS FULL OF SURPRISES, OPEN THEM SLOWLY. — Jackie Mutcheson

just got my ears pierced

What a thrill this was for Emily! After months of us chastising her for her fussy behavior, she worked all summer long on handling difficult situations with more mature behavior. And she did an awesome job in some new and scary situations. So, as a huge surprise to her, we told her that she could get her ears pierced – 18 months earlier than she had expected. It was so much fun to watch her go through all of the emotions of the event!

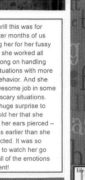

life itself is the proper binge

Pierced Ears
Stephanie Vetne
South Bend, Indiana

Supplies: Cardstock (Bazzill); patterned paper (Creative Imaginations); letter stickers (American Crafts, Arctic Frog, Chatterbox, SEI); sticker accents (7 Gypsies); tape adhesives (Therm O Web); Arial font (Microsoft)

Endless Summer
Shannon Landen
San Antonio, Texas

Supplies: Kraft cardstock; white cardstock (Bazzill); chipboard letters, photo corners (Heidi Swapp); rhinestones (Crafts Etc.); chalk (Deluxe Designs); embroidery thread; image editing software (Adobe)

KAITLIN AMANDA SPENCER
SUMMER 2005
Hot summer days in GRANDMA & GRANDPA's pool
spalsh

SUMMER

Just A Girl
Cheryl Manz, Deerfield, Illinois

Supplies: Cardstock (WorldWin); letter stickers, patterned paper (American Crafts); postcard (Paperchase); mesh (Magic Mesh); patterned transparency (My Mind's Eye); flower (Heidi Swapp); rub-on accents (7 Gypsies, Cactus Pink); word sticker (Making Memories); brads; pen; staples

Mask
Helen McCain, Sun Prairie, Wisconsin

Supplies: Cardstock (WorldWin); patterned paper (BasicGrey, Scenic Route); chipboard letters (K&Co.); flowers (Prima); hole reinforcers (7 Gypsies); lace, linen (unknown); acrylic paint, ribbon (Making Memories); rub-on accents (BasicGrey, My Mind's Eye); stamp (Stampington); tags (Autumn Leaves); embossing paste (Dreamweaver); dye and pigment ink (Ranger, Tsukineko); vario tabs (EK Success); zots adhesive (Therm O Web)

Western Day
Kathleen Summers
Roseville, California

Supplies: Patterned paper (Creative Imaginations, My Mind's Eye); letter stamps (Sugarloaf); acrylic paint; twill; pen

Girlfriends
Karen Burniston
Colorado Springs, Colorado

Supplies: Cardstock (Bazzill); chipboard accents, patterned paper, rub-on accents (My Mind's Eye); photo turns (7 Gypsies); pearl brads (Creative Imaginations); ribbon (Strano); thread

She's taken over her brother's skateboard. It's now her new favorite toy!

Coolskatergirl. ❀

Cool Skater Girl
Mindy Bush
Amman, Idaho

Supplies: Cardstock (WorldWin); patterned paper (Scrapbook.com); rub-on flower (CherryArte)

INTENSE

TRADITION, HAIRCUTS and the TRUTH

Yep another weird TRADITION in our family. At the end of each summer you like to get a Mohawk before football practice starts because you are convinced that it gives you a little attitude on the field. TRUTH: it doesn't. No HAIRCUT in the world is going to give you any attitude because you are too sweet. Right before school starts, it all gets shaved down and evened out. I always explain that football attitude doesn't belong in the classroom. It's a fun tradition just the same and I would rather have a sweet boy than some punk!

Traditions, Haircuts and the Truth
Kitty Foster
Snellville, Georgia

Supplies: Cardstock (WorldWin); patterned paper (CherryArte); chalk ink (Clearsnap); pen; EK Typewriter font (Internet download)

K + D
Kitty Foster
Snellville, Georgia

Supplies: Patterned paper (Creative Imaginations); dye ink (Ranger); Typical Writer font (Internet download)

18 years
4 kids
3 dogs
6 churches
2 swing sets
2 grills
3 apartments
2 rent houses
3 homes
No matter what
it all adds up

ONE Kiss
two sweet months

I met you for the first time and I knew then that my life would never be the same. You were meant to be. Meant to be a part of our family and meant to be my baby. I love you, mom.

Kiss
Mindy Bush
Ammon, Idaho

Supplies: Cardstock (WorldWin); patterned paper (A2Z Essentials); tape runner (Therm O Web); Fabienstem, Steiner fonts (Internet download)

London Calling
Shannon Landen
San Antonio, Texas

Supplies: Cardstock (WorldWin); leather flowers, metal frame (Making Memories); letter stamps (Rusty Pickle); acrylic paint (Delta); rub-on letters (Autumn Leaves); spray paint, temporary spray adhesive (Krylon); dot adhesives (Therm O Web)

For those of you playing along at home, here's the style we consider each layout in this chapter to be.

Back(pack) 2 School: **Eclectic**

Prague: Hip and Trendy

Wishing For Rainbows: Journalistic

Capitol: *Old World Charm*

The Kaleidoscope of My Life:
A tricky one, but we're going with Journalistic

Ouch: **SHAbbY**

Wet & Wild: **Eclectic**

Pierced Ears: Classic

Endless Summer: Anything Goes

Just a Girl: Journalistic

Mask: *Old World Charm*

Western Day: **SHAbbY**

Girlfriends: Classic

Cool Skater Girl: Clean Lines

Traditions, Haircuts and the Truth: Hip and Trendy

Kiss: Clean Lines

K+D: **SHAbbY**

London Calling: Anything Goes

BE COMFORTABLE IN YOUR OWN SKIN, THAT'S THE FIRST RULE.

Isaac Mizrahi

Chapter 3

The Common Denominators

It is important that you know and understand your style before you set about your pages. Why? It's kind of like taking a road trip. You can follow the map, step by step, but understanding where the final destination is makes the trip that much easier. Your goal can be accomplished faster if you have a clear vision of the end result!

For everything

there is a season

Leaves

My son,
I was thinking the other day about the amount of time we have left with you before you one day leave for college. When I stop thinking about it in years and instead think about it in seasons, it puts things in a different perspective. Instead of thinking that you have only 8 more years at home, I thought about how many more winters, springs, falls, and summers we would have and how I need to make the most of them. What will we do? Where will we go and what new traditions will we start? I will need to make time with you a priority and enjoying all the good day to day stuff that we share. It's all good, even when it seems like it's not. It's all a part of life and what God allows and intends for us. Daddy took this picture of us the fall of 2004 and I look forward to the 8 more falls that we can share. For everything there is a season and I'm glad to have this season with you.
Love,
Momma

Autumn

⌜SHAbbY / Journalistic⌝

Kitty deliberately chose rich autumnal hues for this page. Not only did it fit the season of the photo, but they work well with the story she wanted to share with her son about the passing of time.

For Everything There is a Season
Kitty Foster
Snellville, Georgia

Supplies: Cardstock (WorldWin); patterned paper (Cosmo Cricket); transparency (Daisy D's); chalk ink (Clearsnap); jute string; adhesive dots (Therm O Web); AL Charisma font (Autumn Leaves); Bondoni MT font (Internet download)

The next few steps will help you narrow down what it is exactly about each style that you like. Go back over the layouts in the Discovery Zone chapter that you marked and any other layouts that caught your eye. This time, look for the common elements that the layouts share. Following are some characteristics to consider.

Colors

The human eye is naturally drawn to color. Most scrapbookers probably can rattle off their favorite colors quickly. The question then is, "Are you using your favorite colors in your pages?" Many times, we hear, "Well my favorite color to wear is blue, but I tend to scrap with brown." While certain photos demand certain colors (an orange and pink sunset would probably struggle a bit on a bright blue background), it is important to understand the colors that are pleasing to you. As you look back over your favorite page designs, ask yourself these questions: What colors were used in the design? Dark, rich tones? Warm colors? Bright and vivid hues? How do the colors chosen enhance the mood of the design?

How do the colors chosen for these three pages affect you when you look at the pages?

⌐Old World Charm¬

Helen conveys the soft antique feel on her page with warm tones and very worn designs. The viewer feels as if they have stepped back in time just from the colors of this page.

The Sweetest Days
Helen McCain
Sun Prairie, Wisconsin

Supplies: Cardstock (WorldWin); patterned paper (Daisy D's); buttons, crochet trim, metal photo corner and title sticker, staples (Making Memories); letter sticker (K&Co.); rub-on accents (7 Gypsies, BasicGrey); charm (Li'l Davis); lace, rickrack (unknown); printed twill (Autumn Leaves); embossing powder (Ranger); photo corners (Chatterbox); adhesive dots (Therm O Web); adhesive tabs (EK Success)

⌐Eclectic¬

Bright, happy, fun: These are the emotions that Kelly brought out of her photo. The colors can put a smile on just about any face (and so could her son's cute grin!).

Mom's Day
Kelly Goree
Shelbyville, Kentucky

Supplies: Cardstock (WorldWin); chipboard letters, letter stickers, patterned paper (BasicGrey); tag (Avery); ribbon (unknown); epoxy sticker (MOD); pigment ink (Clearsnap); pen; adhesive tape runner (Therm O Web); dimensional adhesive dots; Steelfish font (Internet download)

What statement do the papers make in the pages below?

Wow! These prints just reach out and grab you. They catch your eye and pull you right into the beautiful photos.

Clean Lines

Chocolate
Mindy Bush,
Ammon, Idaho

Supplies: Cardstock (WorldWin); patterned paper, rub-on letters (Arctic Frog); adhesive tape runner (Therm O Web)

Papers

The base to any layout is the background paper. It is the first layer of color or pattern. Determining how to start is sometimes the hardest part of putting the page together. The object here is to implement what you found yourself drawn to while you were in the discovery zone. If you thought you had to start with cardstock for every layout, but all your favorites are patterned backgrounds, it's time to go out on that patterned paper limb and see how you do! What type of papers draw you in? Florals, checks, mostly cardstocks, plaids, stripes, word papers or graphic prints? Do the papers have a light uncluttered feel or do they add to the design of the page in a really dramatic way? Are they part of the design or just used as a placemat for the elements and techniques on the layout?

⟦Journalistic⟧

Cheryl used polka dots in various sizes to give this layout the playful childhood feel that she wanted to evoke.

I Miss You
Cheryl Manz
Deerfield, Illinois

Supplies: Patterned paper (American Crafts, KI Memories, MOD, Scenic Route); chipboard word, letter stickers (Scenic Route); chipboard brackets (Fancy Pants); flowers (Prima); brads; photo corner punch; pen

⟦Classic⟧

Doesn't this text and gaffer's tape take you into the newsroom with Clark Kent? It helps carry the theme of Superman from the photos all the way through to the background in a subtle way.

My Superhero
Stephanie Vetne
South Bend, Indiana

Supplies: Cardstock (WorldWin); patterned paper (American Crafts, K&Co., Mustard Moon, Scenic Route); letter stickers (American Crafts, Arctic Frog, Chatterbox, Making Memories); decorative tape, sticker accents (7 Gypsies); rub-on accents (Autumn Leaves); pen; adhesive tape runner (Therm O Web)

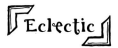

Eclectic

The straight lines of this page keep the focus on the photos, and then the arrow casually leads the eye to the title and journaling. It's a subtle but very effective way to guide the eye through the page.

It's in the Genes
Wendy McKeehan
Batavia, Illinois

Supplies: Cardstock; patterned paper (KI Memories); rub-on letters (7 Gypsies, KI Memories); brad (Bazzill); corner rounder; adhesive dots and tape runner (Therm O Web); Gimme Coffee font (Two Peas in a Bucket)

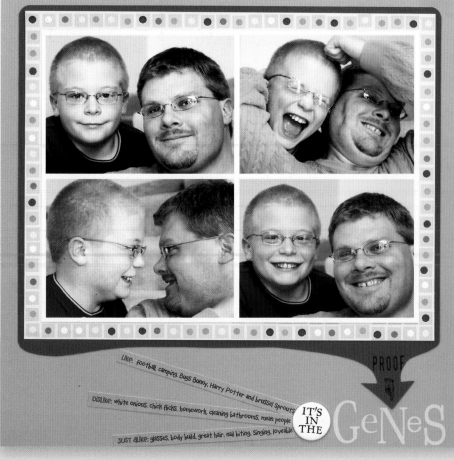

Arrangement

The actual placement of the page elements is a large part of defining your personal style. If you were drawn to the large one-photo page but have been trying to cram all 13 pictures from Timmy's birthday party onto a two-page spread, then it may be time to reevaluate. If the last thing in the world you want to do is enlarge a photo, then your choices in the discovery zone probably show multiple picture pages that are fairly traditional in their layout. If you are drawn to the unique photo options that digital designs afford you, it may be time to sign up for a digi class to learn the steps to creating any size, shape and opacity of photos that you could possibly want. All of these options (and many more) are important to think about in this step.

Here are some questions to ask yourself: How are the elements arranged? How many photos are on the page? Are there enlargements, or just 4" x 6" (10cm x 15cm) photos? Are they placed deliberately or is the display more random? Are the embellishments pulled away from the pictures and brought together in a grouping, or is white space used? Is everything arranged symmetrically or does the page have a softer flow? Is there a visual triangle on the page that helps your eye move around the page?

The placement of elements on the following pages will probably affect you very strongly. Most people don't care for both straight, neat placement and random, hectic patterns. Which side do you see yourself? Or are you a little bit of a rebel who is straddling the lines again…enjoying a little randomness mixed with your straight designs. No worries, an eclectic style is a-ok!

goodbye | hello

goodbye

waistline — morning sickness

sleeping through the night — swollen ankles & hot flashes

being able to see my feet — stretchy pants

laying on my stomach — nightly heartburn

Mountain Dew for breakfast — crippling leg cramps

...and i can't wait! ...

Graphic

The wonderful curve of her hips is a simple but powerful piece to arrange a square layout around. This placement does not make the page feel like it is a box.

Goodbye, Hello
Deena Wuest
Goessel, Kansas

Supplies: Digital background, rectangle, rub-on accents (Designer Digitals); Avant Garde, Dear Joe Four, Eight Track fonts (Internet download)

Anything Goes

Busy, randomness gives this layout a very "teenager" feel. It takes you back to the '80s with the colors, the silk flower wrist corsages and the cassette tape inserts that we all used to tape our favorite songs from our albums. Those were the days!

My Music, My Time
Shannon Landen
San Antonio, Texas

Supplies: Cardstock, chipboard (WorldWin); cassette tape covers (unknown); vellum; letter stickers (Making Memories); letter stamps (Sugarloaf); pigment ink (Clearsnap); rub-on letters (KI Memories); rub-on accents (7 Gypsies); fibers (EK Success); flowers (Doodlebug, Heidi Swapp); glitter (Ranger); lace; rhinestones (My Mind's Eye); staples; pen

Life, as I see it, is one
big unrefundable gift. No
matter how old you are,
where you live, or how
much money you have,
each one of us is given the
same 24 hours each day.
We are free to use them
how we please, but at the
end of the day, there are no
extensions, no exchanges...
no refunds.

I pray that as you grow, you
will live every 24 hours you
are given to it's fullest...that
each day will be a healthy
deposit into this precious
gift we call life. So some day
when you look back over
your time here on earth,
you can say you've lived
a life of no regrets.

Your life is a gift from God.
What you do with it,
is your gift back to Him.
Remember this.

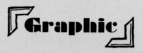

With this layout,
Deena brings us right
in to read the story
she wants to tell.

24
Deena Wuest
Goessel, Kansas

Supplies: Digital patterned paper,
brushes, frames, rub-on accents
(Designer Digitals); 4990810, Myriad
Pro, Steelfish fonts (Internet download)

This huge title makes you want to read more, and the outlined journal boxes also peak the viewer's interest.

Words

What caught your eye? Did you squint to read the pages that had a long story to tell or did you emotionally respond to the simple quote on a page? Consider not only the typography that was used, but also how these pieces of the layout worked in the overall design. If you preferred the layouts with cleverly hidden journaling because you love the idea of having more space for artistic expression, then it's time to play with hinges, hidden tags, and decoratively covered journal boxes. On the other hand, if the words on the page were what drew you to the layout, then a little bit of typography study may be in order to figure out what fonts you really love to see. If you are a strong proponent of hand journaling, then all you need to do is practice a bit before you write on your pages.

A title is another visual attention grabber for some people. Study the pages that you loved to determine the best way to address your pages. You may want a bold title that jumps off the page, or you could prefer a subdued title that is part of a journaling block. Make a note of your preferences and then ask yourself these questions. Where are the title and journaling placed? Does the title draw you in? Is it bold and graphic in style or soft and handwritten? Is the title part of the overall design of the page or does it softly blend into the background? Is the journaling set in a block or is it more random in placement (strips, around the outside of the page, on the photo, etc.)? Are computer fonts used or is the title designed with elements? Are handwritten journaling or fonts used to make the layout feel a bit softer?

How can you tell a Rogers is a Rogers? By their freckles, of course!!!

Megan & Kaitlin are the two grandkids with the most prominent freckles. Yep! They're Rogers!

A Girl without Freckles is like a Night w/o Stars

Shannon does a great job turning this quote into a fun title. It takes a few seconds to read it, but once you have, you just want to continue reading the journaling around the photo.

A Girl Without Freckles
Shannon Landen
San Antonio, Texas

Supplies: Cardstock (WorldWin); acrylic paint (Delta); chipboard letters (Li'l Davis, Making Memories); letter stickers (American Crafts, Doodlebug, K&Co., Making Memories); rub-on letters (Making Memories); chipboard stars (Maya Road); pen

⌈ *Old World Charm* ⌋

Helen has mastered the art of her style by not only her use of vintage colors but with her use of textures and materials. A classic script font gives this layout the perfect old world elegance that the Eiffel tower demands.

Paris
Helen McCain
Sun Prairie, Wisconsin

Supplies: Cardstock (WorldWin); patterned paper (Creative Imaginations, Making Memories); patterned transparencies (K&Co., My Mind's Eye); stamp (Sugarloaf); dye ink (Ranger); ribbon (Making Memories); rub-on accent (7 Gypsies); picture hanger (Daisy D's); ball chain; transparency; adhesive dots, vellum tape (Therm O Web)

Kitty used classic autumnal accents to carry on the theme of her photos. This is the most common use of embellishments.

Enjoying Autumn
Kitty Foster
Snellville, Georgia

Supplies: Cardstock (WorldWin); patterned paper and overlay (Karen Foster); silk leaves (unknown); dye ink; adhesive dots (Therm O Web); spray adhesive (Krylon); Sketchy font (Two Peas in a Bucket)

Embellishments

You will find embellishments to be mostly impulse buys, and therefore a reflection of what you really like. Many times when we buy embellishments we are not thinking of a particular page; rather, we build a page around the embellishment that we love. On the other hand, if you like clean lines, then you probably haven't bought too many embellishments because the "cluttered" look didn't attract you in the first place. This preference will show in the pages you have marked. Are the embellishments used sparingly or are they parts of the overall feel of the page? Do they have an antique, classic, childlike or funky look? Are they part of a coordinated set of products (paper, stickers, chipboard, etc.)? Do they help the overall theme or are they just used for their artistic value? (You know those pages where you throw on a couple extra embellishments just because they are stinkin' cute!) Are they randomly mixed up on the page for a fun look that goes against the theme grain, or does it all match up either in color, shape or size?

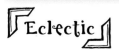

The fun chipboard circles along the wave of journaling give the feel of water that Kelly wanted for these photos. The embellishments soften the hard edges of the photos and carry the eye from the top photos to the bottom of the page.

Boating
Kelly Goree
Shelbyville, Kentucky

Supplies: Cardstock (WorldWin); patterned paper, chipboard circles (Imagination Project); pen; pigment ink (Clearsnap); adhesive dots (Therm O Web)

Groove: a situation suited to one's abilities or interests: NICHE
(yes, we put this definition in here again....it's called emphasis!)

Hip and Trendy

Audrey designed this 8.5" x 11" (22cm x 28cm) page and decided it needed a "little" something, so she layered it onto a 12" x 12" (30cm x 30cm) page of flowers and chunky brads. She created a great frame for her page with the flowers.

Mix It Up
Audrey Neal
Clinton, Kentucky

Supplies: Cardstock (Bazzill); patterned paper (KI Memories); flowers (Doodlebug); brads; letter stickers, plastic letters (Heidi Swapp); rub-on accents (BasicGrey); pigment ink (Clearsnap); polka dot swirl (Scrapbook-Bytes); hole punch; masking tape; notebook paper; pen; ribbon (unknown); zip dry paper glue (Beacon)

So, are the similarities starting to emerge? Do you find yourself consistently drawn toward the same types of pages or do you enjoy elements of several of the designs?

Once you have determined what colors, patterns and embellishments you are drawn to, you will have an easier time designing your pages in a way that is pleasing to you. You will also avoid the pitfalls of wayward product purchases (we all have that "what was I thinking" pile of supplies don't we?) and getting sucked into the latest trends even though they really don't appeal to you.

Now, this is not to say you will always love every page that you do, because we all have designs that look better in our head than they do on paper (or the screen). However, you will have far fewer of these mishaps. It also doesn't mean you will never step out of your "style," but we'll discuss this a bit later. By sticking within a certain area of design, you will become more comfortable with the conceptualization of new page layouts. Once the ball is rolling, you may even get a bit faster at the whole design process. In a word, you will be in a groove.

STYLE HAS NO FORMULA,
BUT IT HAS A SECRET KEY.
IT IS THE EXTENSION OF
YOUR PERSONALITY.

Ernst Haas

Chapter 4

Me, Myself, and Why

Up until now we've worked to discover your
personal style as it applies to outside inspiration.
It is now time to examine your own personal
tastes for insights.

Your style is based on your tastes.

You can't exactly change your tastes…you just like what you like. No matter how hard she tries, Wendy is never going to like army green. She is naturally drawn to different colors, but tastes can also evolve over time. For instance, Wendy's mom abhors the color brown. She never dresses in it, uses it in decorating or picks a piece of furniture that is brown. Honestly, it was surprising that she was willing to serve swiss steak and meatloaf because they were brown! So, Wendy grew up not liking brown either—that was part of her "taste history." As she has gotten older, and moved out on her own, she now appreciates the color brown and will use it here and there in her decorating and scrapbooking (although you probably won't catch her wearing a chocolate brown sweater!). That evolution took some time. This applies to clothing, home décor as well as your artistic design style. Becoming more aware of your tastes will help to streamline the discovery process.

Now it's time to take this discovery technique and apply it to your own pages. Check out your personal online gallery or just flip through your albums and repeat this process. Armed with style knowledge you may begin to look at your pages in a new light. What is it about your pages that you really love? And we need more than just that your children are adorable, your dog is goofy or that you have the best family in the world! Is there a common thread that runs through the design of your layouts? What about the pages are you not enamored with…can you see what is missing? Do your pages match the style that you want them to be or do you need to tweak them a bit? This is all a part of the discovery process and without discovery, how can you develop a personal style?

With all the discussion about product and styles we tend to forget one crucial element; ourselves. We are focused on others; on what they do, on what the newest papers look like, what the latest embellishment craze is or what is the hip trend that everyone is following. What we really need to do is focus inward. We need to figure out what motivates us in the first place (story, photos, products, techniques, etc.). When it comes to developing our own style, what matters most is finding out who we are, what we like and what we dislike. Developing a personal style is not copying someone else's style. Developing a personal style is finding out who you are and what makes your work the extension of your personality. There's nothing wrong with being influenced by others, or even duplicating (i.e. scraplifting) them as part of the learning process. But the goal is to take it a step further and add that special something that is original. Find that one element or design accent that is all about you.

It takes time to develop a personal style; it does not come overnight. Anything worth your effort is worth your time. If you wanted to be on the Olympic swim team, you would have to practice—a lot. This is no different. Scrapbooking once a month will not help you in your goal of style discovery. You will need to do consistent work until you hit that sweet spot…your groove. It's about how you combine choices and how you express emotions in your art.

Here are a few suggestions of additional things you can do that may help you on your quest for personal style along with a few more inspiring layouts (because it's all about the eye candy in an idea book…don't you agree?).

A good style: nothing can be added to it; neither can anything be taken from it.

RALPH WALDO EMERSON

Attend classes

Knowledge is power. Take a class and learn a new technique or design a page in a totally new way. You may or may not like what you have created (maybe alcohol inks smeared on the table and then rubbed onto paper are not your thing) but the knowledge of that will help you as you shape your style.

⌜Anything Goes⌝

Shannon made these clever flowers from Spirograph drawings. After they were cut out, she watercolored them to add a soft color palette to her layout. Can't say that I've ever seen Spirograph flowers on a scrapbook page before!

Sisters
Shannon Landen
San Antonio, Texas

Supplies: Cardstock (WorldWin); spiral shape templates (Klutz); clay letters (Li'l Davis); notebook paper; journaling stamps (Autumn Leaves); decorative tape, metal clips (Making Memories); paper flowers (Making Memories, Prima); buttons (Doodlebug); chipboard hearts, floral sequins (Heidi Swapp); epoxy stickers, metal word (K&Co.); ribbon (Maya Road); rickrack (All My Memories, Making Memories); decorative scissors; dye ink (Ranger); pen; adhesive (Therm O Web)

⌜Hip and Trendy⌝

Wendy attended a class and learned all about alcohol inks. She loved the class and making a mess, but her girlfriend was not as enamored with the technique (or the mess!). Both learned something more about their style after taking the class.

Party of One
Wendy McKeehan
Batavia, Illinois

Supplies: Cardstock (WorldWin); notebook paper; rub-on letters (CherryArte, Imagination Project); transparency; alcohol ink (Ranger); rhinestone word (Me & My Big Ideas); flowers (Heidi Swapp); rhinestone brads (Making Memories); adhesive dots, tape runner (Therm O Web)

Seek out a Mentor

If you really admire and respect someone's work, ask them if you could be their student. Sometimes, just learning how they go through the design process is enough to help you get comfortable with your own thought process. Scraplifting their work can also help you to understand how they go about creating their art. We find that when we start to scraplift a page, it inevitably ends up looking different than the original. As we go along, our tastes come into play and we veer off course and end up with a page that was inspired instead. And if you are lucky enough to find a mentor that lives locally, you may even discover a new favorite coffee drink or the best place to buy great shoes in addition to gleaning some of their design expertise!

『Eclectic』

Shine
Wendy McKeehan
Batavia, Illinois

Supplies: Cardstock (WorldWin); patterned paper (Making Memories); letter stickers (Mustard Moon); buttons (unknown); pen

『Eclectic』

Wendy is a long-time admirer of Kelly's work, so she asked Kelly if she could scraplift "The Lucky One" layout for this chapter. Wendy used a similar large shape for her page and ended up with an interpretation that, while similar, certainly has its own unique qualities as well.

Lucky One
Kelly Goree
Shelbyville, Kentucky

Supplies: Cardstock (Bazzill); patterned paper, chipboard circle (Scenic Route); chipboard letters (CherryArte); chipboard diamonds, rub-on letters (Heidi Swapp); pigment ink (Clearsnap); pen; adhesive tape runner (Therm O Web); Edwardian Script title font (Microsoft)

Beautiful

FRESH
COUNTRY
EGGS

At Sues farm the
summer of 2004
We had fun taking
photos. We got some
beautiful shots. Grm. Wi.

Don't be afraid to fail

Even people who you admire or who seem to be very comfortable in their style still create some dud pages. It happens to us all. The difference is how they handle it. Sometimes, despite our best efforts, the page is just not going to be as good as we envisioned. It's OK. Finish it off, put it in a page protector and move on. (Bet you were hoping for some ugly layouts in this section, weren't you? Get real!)

Old World Charm

Helen played with a new technique on this page to give the background a great texture. She spread embossing paste on part of the background with a palette knife, then she used walnut ink mixed with some modeling paste and spread that over part of the background to create the rich texture shown.

Beautiful
Helen McCain
Sun Prairie, Wisconsin

Supplies: Cardstock (Bazzill); patterned paper (Imagination Project); acrylic paint, fabric tape, rickrack, trim (Making Memories); fabric (Junkitz); rub-on title (Scenic Route); twill (EK Success); charm (Maya Road); flower (Prima); dye and pigment ink (Ranger, Tsukineko); embossing paste (Liquitex); photo corners (Chatterbox); pen; adhesive dots (Therm O Web)

See your work from a different point of view

Before a person posts a layout on an online gallery, they have to either take a good digital picture of their layout or scan it. If you scan your layout, take time to look at it on the computer screen—it may help you to see it differently. Just like when you look through online galleries and a layout thumbnail catches your eye, look at your own layouts in thumbnail size and see if they catch *your* eye.

Elizabeth and Curly go every-where together. They are a team – they have mastered two years of preschool, scary monsters, thunderstorms, upset tummies, hurt feelings, and even a hospital stay together. Now, they are both off to full-day kindergarten at SCS. There have been already been a few tears and lots and lots of hugs, but I know that, together, they will do just fine. Oh, and um.. Curly....thank you from Mommy.

Classic

Thank You, Curly!
Stephanie Vetne
South Bend, Indiana

Supplies: Cardstock (WorldWin); patterned paper (BasicGrey); letter stickers (American Crafts); circle punch; corner rounder; adhesive tape runner (Therm O Web); Arial font (Microsoft)

Laughter, tears, and giggles.

she runs on **Pure emotion**

NOTHING ARTIFICIAL

My saige is a master of emotions.

Clean Lines

Pure Emotion
Mindy Bush
Ammon, Idaho

Supplies: Cardstock (WorldWin); patterned paper (A2Z Essentials, My Mind's Eye); chipboard, flower (Heidi Swapp); adhesive tape runner (Therm O Web)

white buffalo

Buffalo Crossing, Eminence, Kentucky

Eclectic

White Buffalo
Kelly Goree
Shelbyville, Kentucky

Supplies: Cardstock (Bazzill); patterned paper (Chatterbox); chipboard accent (CherryArte); stamps (Technique Tuesday); pigment ink; hole punch; pen

On Friday, June 3, 2005, a miracle happened and only 10 minutes from my home. On this day, a pure white buffalo calf made her entrance into the world at Buffalo Crossing Ranch in Eminence, Kentucky.

With odds estimated at more than 1 in 10 million, experts with the National Buffalo Association had believed the gene needed to produce a white calf had been lost when the buffalo was nearly driven to extinction. So that makes the little calf's birth an event rare and special as it is. But that's only part of the story. Because for the Lakota Sioux and the entire Sioux Nation, a female white buffalo calf is the most sacred thing you can encounter, a prophecy come true. A calf such as this is the embodiment of their "White Buffalo Woman", the one who brought to them the Sacred Pipe and taught them the ways of the earth and heaven.

Local and National news covered our blessed event and hundreds of people made a pilgrimage to the Ranch to see this newborn calf. Many tribes held prayer vigils and left tokens and sacred offerings for her. These photos were taken when she was just a little over a month old during a family trip made to Buffalo Crossing to witness this miracle for ourselves. July, 2005

there has never been a day

when I have not been proud of you, I said, though some days I'm louder about other stuff so it's easy to miss that." Brian Andreas

Challenge yourself

Sometimes the greatest challenges come from within, when you challenge yourself with an assignment. It can be a product challenge (you must use plaid paper, like Stephanie did in her layout on the next page), it can be a photo challenge (scrapbook an old high school picture of yourself), or it could be a technique challenge (actually *use* that new chartreuse embossing powder you bought!). Try doing something you've never seen done. That is where innovation lives…on the outskirts of our creative boundaries. Reach for it!

Hip and Trendy

There has Never Been a Day
Audrey Neal
Clinton, Kentucky

Supplies: Cardstock (WorldWin); chipboard coaster, patterned paper (Imagination Project); letter stickers (American Crafts); rub-on accents (Cactus Pink); epoxy stickers, square brads (Around the Block); rhinestones (unknown); pen; pigment ink (Clearsnap); zip dry paper glue (Beacon)

I love these two pictures of you and your little brother. It took some getting used to – you had always been the little sister. So, becoming the big sister took some time. But, you have truly taken over the role with gusto. These pictures show so well how much you love Andrew. So protective and so willing to be patient with him and teach him how to do so many things. You seem to really love the role of teacher and mentor – and you have such a gentle guiding hand. I am so proud of you.

⟦Classic⟧

Big Sister
Stephanie Vetne
South Bend, Indiana

Supplies: Cardstock (WorldWin); patterned paper, letter stickers (Mustard Moon); rub-on accents (BasicGrey); dye ink (Ranger); photo turns (7 Gypsies); adhesive tape runner (Therm O Web); Times New Roman font (Microsoft)

⟦SHAbbY⟧

San Francisco
Kathleen Summers
Roseville, California

Supplies: Cardstock, chipboard (WorldWin); patterned paper (Creative Imaginations); canvas flowers, letter stamps (Autumn Leaves); acrylic paint; patterned transparencies, rub-on accents (My Mind's Eye); decorative brad (Making Memories); button (Dress It Up); dye and solvent ink (Ranger, Tsukineko); fabric scraps; pen; adhesive foam, vellum adhesive (Therm O Web)

Practice!

Yes, this seems trite, but the truth is that it is almost impossible to discover your personal style if you don't actually scrapbook! Now, we are not suggesting scrapping at the expense of your laundry and home cooked meals (tempting as that may be), but working on a page a week at least will keep you fresh and in a rhythm.

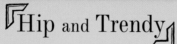

⌈Hip and Trendy⌋

Random Advice
Audrey Neal
Clinton, Kentucky

Supplies: Cardstock (WorldWin); chipboard accents, patterned paper, rub-on accents (Urban Lily); chipboard letters, journaling accents, plastic accent (Heidi Swapp); glitter glue; pigment ink (Clearsnap); staples; pen; adhesive foam (Therm O Web); zip dry paper glue (Beacon)

『Journalistic』

No Turning Back
Cheryl Manz
Deerfield, Illinois

Supplies: Patterned paper (American Crafts, Fancy Pants); patterned transparency (My Mind's Eye); letter stickers (Heidi Swapp); brads; notebook paper; sandpaper; staples; pen

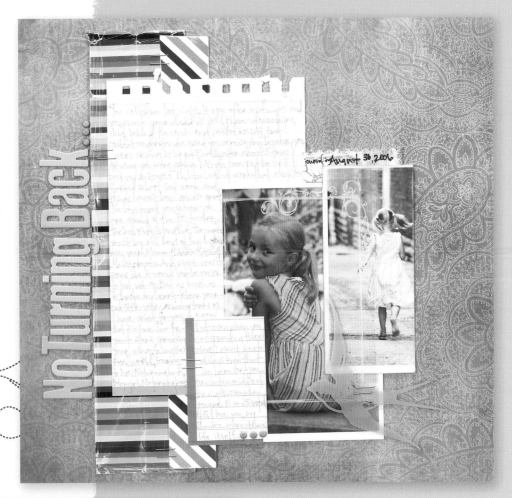

『SHAbbY/Journalistic』

Finding Your Voice
Kitty Foster
Snellville, Georgia

Supplies: Patterned paper (Creative Imaginations); rub-on letters (7 Gypsies, BasicGrey); silk flowers (unknown); dye ink (Ranger); thread; Times New Roman font (Microsoft)

To my daughter,

High school is approaching and with this new exciting adventure will come new challenges. One of the hardest challenges will be finding your voice. Oh you don't have a problem giving your opinion about where we go to eat or what you want to wear, this is different. A voice is what tells your testimony or asks questions that need to be asked even if others are afraid to. It can be a salve to another hurting heart but can be strong and defend the weak. Your voice will make sense out of your life and will show you your feelings and how you will deal with them. It can bring you honor or embarrassment but will always bring you truth. Your voice can encourage others to stand up for what is right and to face the same challenges as you with grace. Finding your voice will take time but I know and trust that you will find it. Your voice is independent from those around you and should never be one that is pressured by the opinions of others. Finding your voice is the first step in being a leader. You will achieve many great things!

It was a summer day like any other. You and Savanna were playing outside on the slip n slide and I was contentedly watching from the sidelines. Out of the corner of my eye, I noticed that Savanna had unhooked the hose and was aiming right for you. Before I could stop her...SPLASH...you were drenched from head to toe.

{It was then that it happened}

REALIZATION *reluctant*

Instead of crying and running to me for protection you turned to Savanna, giggled, and started chasing her with a stick. It was in that moment that I realized something I've been trying to deny for a while now. I realized that you are no longer my baby, but a little boy.

Apparently, a little boy who can hold his own.

⌈Graphic⌋

Reluctant Realization
Deena Wuest
Goessel, Kansas

Supplies: Digital arrows, circle stamps and circle scribbles (Designer Digitals); Century Gothic, Impact fonts (Microsoft); Jane Austen font (Internet download)

One of the best parts of our neighborhood are the kids. On just our block alone there are six children within two years of Karl and Emma's age. On Halloween the gang set out Trick-or-Treating together and made short work of the entire neighborhood. Too bad they don't show the same pep when it comes to walking to school!

THe NEiGHBORHOOD GANG FROM LeFt to RiGHt: KARL, ZACK, JANESSA, PATRICK, KAiLYNN, EMMA

BOO!   BOO!   BOO!

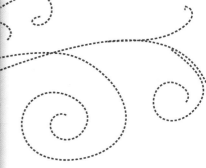

⌈SHAbbY⌋

Halloween 2005
Karen Burniston
Colorado Springs, Colorado

Supplies: Cardstock, chipboard circles (Bazzill); patterned paper (Heidi Grace, My Mind's Eye, Paperwhite); die-cut paperclip (QuicKutz); rubber stamps (unknown); measuring tape, ribbon (Wal-Mart)

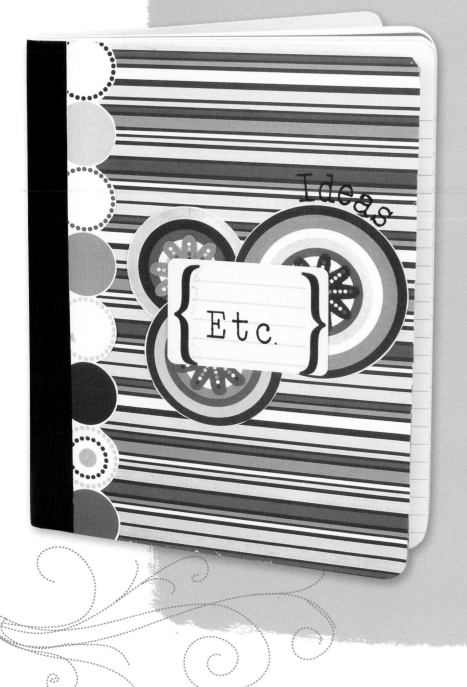

Idea Journal

This is a great time to start keeping a notebook or journal that you can fill with inspirational ideas, sketches or colors. Every time you see something that catches your eye, jot it down. Always go with your gut—you have to trust your responses and impressions. Don't second guess. Sometimes this exercise can ignite the spark of imagination and set you on your way! This notebook will help you in several ways, it will help you get even closer to discovering your own style, and on days when the mojo is low and ideas aren't flowing—it will be a welcomed fount of inspiration. Sometimes just doing some paper crafting with your supplies is all the inspiration you need, so grab a blank notebook and make it your own like Kitty did.

Classic

Ideas Etc. Notebook
Kitty Foster
Snellville, Georgia

Supplies: Patterned paper, coaster and rub-on accents (Imagination Project); chalk ink (Clearsnap); notebook

By now, you should have a pretty good idea of where you fit on the style spectrum.

Maybe you see yourself fitting into one of our definitions perfectly. Maybe you are one of those "straddlers" who sees themselves somewhere between two different definitions. And maybe you think we are nuts and have a completely different personal definition of your style. Any of those choices is fine. You should have a pretty good understanding about your scrapbook DNA, so it's time to work your style so you can get comfortable in your groove.

Work it sister!

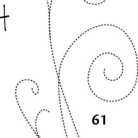

Chapter 5

Out of the Rut and Into the Groove

Not every groove is a good one. Sometimes when we continue to do the same thing over and over we are stuck, just like being stuck in a groove in the road. When you are in a rut, you lack inspiration, and whatever it is you're doing becomes habit and gets boring—fast! Inspiration can not be forced. What can you do when you are all tapped out, have nothing more to give and want to do a project? Inspiration hits you when you least expect it and while you are waiting for it to hit, there are several steps that you can take to help the process along. Many times it is learning to look at the same thing in a different way.

When you go to your favorite mall, you probably always park in the same place. Maybe you have a favorite department store door that you park next to so you remember that your car is near the door by the purses. Or maybe you like to enter near the food court every time you go so you can have easy access to an ice cream cone or a mocha latte. Whatever your choice, it is part of your routine. Sometimes we need to break from tradition and park somewhere new. Yes, this is a silly example, but you get the point! Breaking up your shopping routine will help you see your favorite stores in a new way. So it is with your creativity. Sometimes we just need to shake things up a bit to get your groove back. Here are a few suggestions to help you get out of a creative rut.

Try something completely different

Have you ever thought about trying your hand at a totally different look? Something that would really stretch you? We challenged a few scrapbookers to do just that. We asked each of them to do a layout in a style we felt was their polar opposite. Some found the challenge easy and inspiring; others really struggled to complete it. Next time you are feeling stagnant, try this exercise. You may be very surprised at the results!

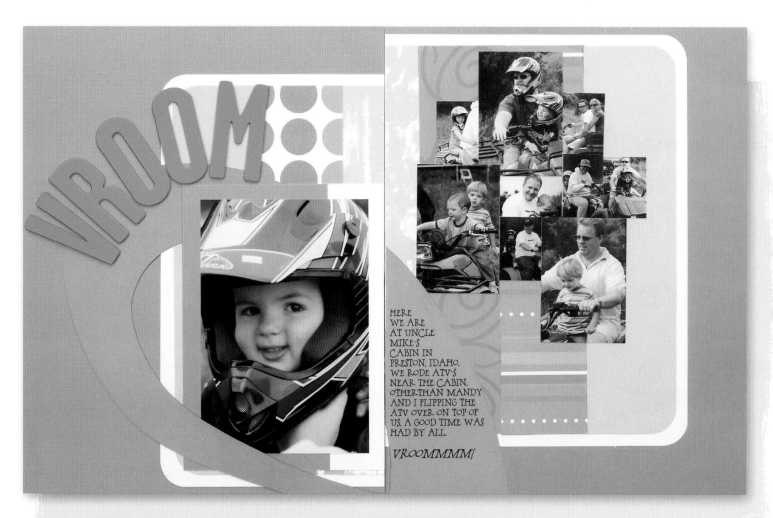

My approach to scrapbooking is Anything Goes! I like to dabble in every style that catches my interest. Therefore, creating a graphic style page for the challenge was fun and easy. The biggest challenge was figuring out how to print the journaling text as a cohesive part of the page, as I usually handwrite most of my journaling. I resolved that issue by printing on cardstock, and I was pleased with the results.

{Shannon}

Vroom
Shannon Landen
San Antonio, Texas

Supplies: Cardstock (Bazzill, WorldWin); patterned paper (CherryArte, Creative Imaginations, Paper Studio); acrylic paint, chipboard letters (Making Memories); corner rounder; Bosshole font (Internet download)

Because my normal style is more bright and funky, it was a little rough doing a layout using the more subtle colors and aging techniques of a Shabby style. It took me a little longer to figure out how to get everything to work together, but in the end, I feel like I was able to bring a little of my own style to the page and mix the two together to make it shabby and yet still my own.

{Cheryl}

Growing Together
Cheryl Manz
Deerfield, Illinois

Supplies: Patterned paper, chipboard word (Scenic Route); letter stickers (American Crafts); decorative tape, journaling tag, sticker accents (7 Gypsies); rhinestones (My Mind's Eye); rub-on accents (7 Gypsies, BasicGrey); ruler sticker (Li'l Davis); sandpaper; pen

My style is Classic and fairly symmetrical. For this assignment, I was told to use an Eclectic style. While it was a bit daunting to break out of my mold, it was also very liberating. I used a lot more embellishments than I would normally have used, and the end result is fun and playful. I love the way that this great photo of my daughter is still the focal point of the layout.

{Stephanie}

Biker Chic
Stephanie Vetne
South Bend, Indiana

Supplies: Cardstock (WorldWin); patterned paper, ribbon slide, sticker accent (Making Memories); letter stickers (Making Memories, Doodlebug); flowers (Bazzill); rhinestones, rub-on accents (My Mind's Eye); stamp (Autumn Leaves); pigment ink (Tsukineko); ribbon (Making Memories, Maya Road); corner rounder; decorative scissors; pen; adhesive dots, tape and tape runner (Therm O Web)

My natural style is Shabby and I was challenged to do an Anything Goes layout. I didn't hold back with using a variety of patterned paper and stamps and took the freedom to include a piece of memorabilia (a business card from the restaurant where we were that night) in the midst of it all. Since my pages tend to be linear, it was really fun to let myself go and just lay something down as I put my hands on it. It indeed was very freeing to make a page in this style, and I had a blast!

{Kathleen}

Good
Kathleen Summers
Roseville, California

Supplies: Cardstock (WorldWin); patterned paper (BasicGrey, Imagination Project, Paper House); stamps (Sugarloaf); border sticker, brad (Making Memories); buttons (SEI); chipboard flower (Heidi Swapp); paper flowers (Fancy Pants); photo transparency (My Mind's Eye); rub-on accents (Junkitz, My Mind's Eye); silk flowers (craft supply store); wax (7 Gypsies); pen

My style was called Eclectic in this book—if it feels right for the photos I have to scrap, I like to go for it. I do play around with many different styles and trends as they come along, and Clean Lines, which is what I was challenged to do, is one of my favorites. It is great particularly for photos that might be otherwise busy or colorful and that's why I loved using it here.

{Kelly}

Space Cowboy
Kelly Goree
Shelbyville, Kentucky

Supplies: Cardstock (Bazzill); letter stickers, patterned paper (Paper Loft); chipboard letters (BasicGrey); rub-on letters (My Mind's Eye); chipboard (WorldWin); embroidery floss; pen; adhesive tape runner (Therm O Web)

~~Colic~~
~~Angel~~ baby.

You are such a perfect, wonderful, addition to our family. I love this photo of you sleeping soundly because it doesn't happen very often and I try to treasure it when it does. You see, my poor little sweetheart, you have a touch of colic and it has made you cry alot. I feel so sorry for you and the pain you seem to be in. It's such a hopeless feeling. I want to help you, comfort you, but there doesn't seem to be much that I can do to relieve your pain. So, I'll continue to rock you and hold you as much as I can so that you know how loved you are and hope and pray that it goes away soon.

mine.

My natural style is Clean Line, and I was asked to do a Journalistic page. At the time I was dealing with a colicy baby and decided that would be the theme of my layout. I designed the layout around the journaling, and found that by starting with the journaling in mind first, I was able to create a layout that was more meaningful and thoughtful for future readers. It made me realize just how important our story is, and I want to do better at telling it.

{Mindy}

Colic Baby
Mindy Bush
Ammon, Idaho

Supplies: Cardstock (WorldWin); patterned paper (A2Z Essentials, KI Memories); chipboard letters (Heidi Swapp); ribbon (American Crafts, BasicGrey, Strano); brad; corner rounder; adhesive dots and tape (Therm O Web)

Old World Charm is the style I am drawn to most naturally. My personal style has fluctuated during the last couple of years from more modern to clean lines. While I can learn and use elements from those styles or from the Classic style, like I did here, I always seem to go back to the incorporation of Old World.

{Helen}

Erin all dressed up as Mulan for Halloween, 2002. Sun Prairie.

Mulan
Helen McCain
Sun Prairie, Wisconsin

Supplies: Cardstock (Bazzill); patterned paper (Daisy D's); letter stickers (Making Memories); fabric tabs (Scrapworks); ribbon (Mrs. Grossman's); rub-on accents (BasicGrey, Daisy D's); silk flowers (unknown); pen; adhesive dots (Therm O Web); adhesive tabs (EK Success)

From my Clean/Eclectic natural style I was challenged to do a Hip and Trendy design. As a trend follower (not a trendsetter), I looked to outside inspiration for my layout. A wonderful graphic poster pushed me to create a layout using color combos that I don't normally choose. I ended up really enjoying the result after my initial trepidation of this style.

{Wendy}

Laugh Out Loud
Wendy McKeehan
Batavia, Illinois

Supplies: Cardstock; patterned paper (American Crafts); digital frames (Designer Digitals); chipboard letters (Scenic Route); rub-on letters (Li'l Davis); chipboard arrow (Heidi Swapp); narrative film strip (Creative Imaginations); negative strips; image editing software; Cookie Dough, Fragile, Grandpa, Just Plain Little, Silly Fill-in, Stand Tall fonts (Two Peas in a Bucket); Professor, Rollercoaster, Wazoo fonts (Internet download)

Take a break

You have gathered your products, photos and even have the journaling in your head. You have stared at it so long you are starting to feel light-headed, and you are getting nowhere. Forget about it for awhile. Get away from the layout for an afternoon or a day. Go to the movies, play with your kids or work on something that uses the non-creative side of your brain like crossword puzzles. Sleep on it overnight. Then come back and try again. Forced creativity will most definitely look like you pushed it and will usually feel like you pushed too hard.

Change your routine

If you usually look for a picture that inspires you and then find products and finally write your journaling, maybe it's time to mix up your routine. Maybe you need to start with a brand new paper or embellishment and go on a hunt for the perfect photo to go with it. Maybe there's a story you know that you need to record soon so you don't forget it. Start with the words and then find a photo that expresses the mood in your journaling.

Talk about it

In a perfect world, we'd all have a creative muse—a person that we really connect with artistically. If you don't have one, you will have to find someone else that you can talk to about your ideas (or lack of!). This can be someone who isn't even a scrapbooker at all. Wendy often calls her sister for inspiration or when she needs to brainstorm. Nikki is not a scrapbooker, but she knows Wendy better than anyone and is an extremely talented artist in her own right, so her ideas are usually right on target. Sometimes another person will see what you can't and will bring fresh eyes to the project.

My style for this book is Hip and Trendy, so I was challenged to complete a layout using the Shabby style. The soft colors and patterns of this style just don't have enough pop for me normally. I asked myself: What are the basics of this style? What can I do to shake those basics up a bit? So I used stitching, but made it trendier by cutting out the scalloped border before stitching it to the page. I added buttons and ribbon but used them to create funky flowers.

{Audrey}

Pout
Audrey Neal
Clinton, Kentucky

Supplies: Cardstock (Bazzill); patterned paper (Dream Street); chipboard letters (K&Co.); glitter flowers (Melissa Frances); buttons (Autumn Leaves); lace (Making Memories); ribbon (unknown); edge distresser (Heidi Swapp); thread; pen; zip dry paper glue (Beacon)

Participate in challenges

Many online sites offer challenges. You can be inspired by many of them or none. If you aren't inspired, then have no fear, new challenges are generally posted each month. The challenges vary from trying a new product or technique to interpreting a specific subject matter. You can also just challenge yourself. Maybe you want to use a new stamp or try a new technique. Maybe you need to do a page to wrap up a family album, or maybe you just want to use something out of your stash because you are tired of thumbing past it on the way to something else. The following pages were inspired by some type of challenge mentioned above.

「Journalistic」

Cheryl frequently runs challenges on her blog using random products. For this page she challenged herself to use at least three different patterned papers and to doodle with a white pen.

You Stand Tall
Cheryl Manz
Deerfield, Illinois

Supplies: Cardstock (WorldWin); patterned paper (American Crafts); chipboard letters (Heidi Swapp); chipboard accents (Fancy Pants); rub-on accents (7 Gypsies); pen

「SHAbbY」

Kathleen's challenge was to incorporate preprinted products into her shabby design style. These My Mind's Eye title blocks were the perfect accents for her page once she took a little sandpaper to them. They really work but do not take anything away from her wonderful photos.

Mi Amore
Kathleen Summers
Roseville, California

Supplies: Patterned paper (BasicGrey, Melissa Frances, My Mind's Eye); title and word accents (My Mind's Eye); chipboard hearts, photo corners (Heidi Swapp); pins, velvet ribbon (Making Memories); rub-on accents (7 Gypsies); clip accent (EK Success); adhesive foam (Therm O Web); dye ink (Ranger); sandpaper; thread

Old World Charm

As a fun way to mix up her layout, Helen wrote several products onto small pieces of paper and randomly chose three for her page. She had to use lace, rub-ons and a transparency.

Cowgirl
Helen McCain
Sun Prairie, Wisconsin

Supplies: Cardstock (WorldWin); patterned paper, rhinestones (My Mind's Eye); fabric (Junkitz); fabric tabs (Scrapworks); rub-on accents (BasicGrey); foam stamp, trim (Making Memories); ribbon (Mrs. Grossman's); sticker accent (Cosmo Cricket); transparency; silk flowers, wheat (unknown); acrylic paint; pen; adhesive tabs (EK Success); adhesive dots and tape runner (Therm O Web)

Classic

Sometimes it's challenge enough to use only one product line. Stephanie's challenge was to create a two-page spread using Scenic Route papers and chipboard accents.

My Granny Bike
Stephanie Vetne
South Bend, Indiana

Supplies: Cardstock (WorldWin); chipboard accents, patterned paper (Scenic Route); letter stickers (American Crafts); sticker accents (Sweetwater); rub-on accents (Maya Road); pen; adhesive tape runner (Therm O Web)

Classic

As one of the classic scrapbookers in this book, Karen was asked to use a classic product on her page...vellum.

The Big Tooth Escape
Karen Burniston
Colorado Springs, Colorado

Supplies: Cardstock (WorldWin); patterned paper (American Crafts); vellum; rubber stamps (De Creatie); rhinestone brad (Creative Imaginations); chalk; flower (unknown); thread; pen

Clean Lines

Mindy makes it her goal to always end the year with a recap page. It is perfect for sending to the family and also works well as the last page of her scrapbook album.

The Bush Family
Mindy Bush
Ammon, Idaho

Supplies: Cardstock (WorldWin); patterned paper (BasicGrey); adhesive tape runner (Therm O Web); Fabienstem, Steiner fonts (Internet download)

Children are the flowers of life.

Eclectic

Wendy was inspired by a graphic t-shirt hanging in a store window. She sketched the t-shirt (because she was too cheap to buy it!) and translated the general design onto her layout.

Children are the Flowers
Wendy McKeehan
Batavia, Illinois

Supplies: Cardstock (WorldWin); patterned paper (Stemma); patterned transparency, tag (My Mind's Eye); rhinestones; pen; adhesive squares (3L)

Clean up your space

When the mojo isn't flowing, maybe it's time to clean up your scrap area and rediscover some of your supplies. If you are one of those anal people who have pristine scrap spaces (overachievers!), then maybe it's time for a little reorganization of your supplies. You may discover a new combination of elements that would look great on your next layout.

Get back to basics

What aspects of your style do you really love? Is it your use of patterned paper? Or your love of hip color combinations? Try doing a quick page using some of your favorites. Sometimes you just need to keep it simple for a few layouts and then you will be inspired to go back out on your creativity limb.

Listen to your body clock

Some of us are at our best first thing in the morning. Others are burning the midnight oil well into the wee hours of the night. Trying to be creative "off schedule" can cause your groove to get up and go. Take Kitty, for example. She calls herself a scrapbook vampire. If the sun is out, her creativity is gone. She knows this and makes sure to carve out creative time after the sun goes down.

Of course, we are not all lucky enough to coordinate our creativity clock with our free time every time we want to do something creative. But there are still things you can do with your free time, such as organizing your scrap space, doing some inspirational shopping (we find that this activity works well whether it's early in the morning, during the afternoon or late at night!) or you could work on journaling. Journaling is a skill that uses the other side of our brains, so separating the writing of the story from the assembly of the layout is not a bad idea.

Seek inspiration

If your comfort zone is Shabby, and Graphic layouts are all the rage, finding inspiration for your style in the world of scrapbooking may be tough. If so, seek out inspiration from non-scrapbooking sources: home and fashion magazines, movies, books, all those catalogs that come to your house (a good excuse to keep them around!). Don't feel the need to jump on someone else's bandwagon. Everyone appreciates originality! Marching is fun as long as the beat is your own drum. The following pages were inspired by things outside the realm of scrapbooking. We know there is inspiration all around, we just have to train our eyes to see it.

『Clean Lines』

Kitty came back from her weekend in New York inspired by the sights, sounds and hustle-bustle of the city. She used bright colors, arrows for movement and busy photos to convey her feelings onto her page.

New York
Kitty Foster
Snellville, Georgia

Supplies: Cardstock (WorldWin); patterned paper, chipboard accents and letters (Scenic Route); chalk ink (Clearsnap)

I entered an essay contest about friendship for Spiegel catalog. To my shock, Shannan and I found out that we had won the trip to New York! We had an incredible time. We stayed at the Bryant Park Hotel, rode in a dozen taxis, went to Times Square, saw 2 Broadway shows, had a day at the spa, visited Ground Zero, went to many wonderful restaurants and saw a parade in China Town! It was an opportunity of a lifetime!

『SHAbbY』

Using an antique ornament for inspiration, Kathleen captured the vintage softness in her layout with lace, warm colors and script fonts.

Christmas Dreams
Kathleen Summers
Roseville, California

Supplies: Cardstock (WorldWin); metal tabs, patterned paper (Karen Foster); lace (Making Memories); rub-on accent (BasicGrey); dye ink, stamp (Sugarloaf); photo corner (Heidi Swapp); fabric, ribbon, rickrack (unknown); sandpaper; pen

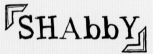

Hip and Trendy

While flipping through her favorite magazine, Audrey was drawn to the use of hands in an ad to emphasize a focal point. She recreated this look on her page with handmade accents (no pun intended).

Like Father, Like Daughter
Audrey Neal
Clinton, Kentucky

Supplies: Cardstock (Bazzill); patterned paper (Fontwerks); chipboard letters, journaling arrow, metal tabs, plastic letters (Heidi Swapp); letter stickers (unknown); pigment ink (Clearsnap); pen; zip dry adhesive (Beacon); Impact font (Microsoft)

SHAbbY

Helen drove past a billboard that caught her eye every day on her way to her daughter's school. She finally made a note of it so she could create this page that was inspired by the design and title.

Girl With Flare
Helen McCain
Sun Prairie, Wisconsin

Supplies: Cardstock (WorldWin); patterned paper and transparency, rub-on accents (My Mind's Eye); ribbon (BasicGrey, Making Memories); button, lace trim (Making Memories); flower (Prima); dye ink (Ranger); white wash paint (Krylon); adhesive dots and tape runner (Therm O Web)

Now that you've mixed it up a bit and reenergized your style, the next time you're at the mall, feel free to park by the food court again so you can get your ice cream cone or mocha latte on the way out the door!

STYLE IS THE PERFECTION OF
A POINT OF VIEW.

Richard Eberhart

Chapter 6

Get Inspired

Gazing through online galleries reminds me of jeans shopping. I have to try on dozens before I find the right one that is me and is a comfortable fit! The gallery can be the same—many wonderful things to look at, but not all will be the right fit for you. There are so many ways to look at a gallery. You can sip a latte while you window shop or go at it with a plan in mind. If the planned route is what you desire, take notes as you look, and jot down your favorite color schemes, photo placement or even a new technique. Regardless of your plan or style, this gallery is a great tool for inspiration!

Larissa
Cheerful: Greek

Life is never dull with your adventurous and restless spirit. You are always on the move and seeking a new challenge to pit your wits against. Being in touch with nature you love the outdoors. You have keen intuition and a desire for knowledge and you can be something of a crusader. When you apply discipline and tenacity to your energetic mind then leadership positions are easily available to you.

⟦Clean Lines⟧

Larissa
Janneke Smit
Agoura, California

Supplies: Cardstock (Bazzill, Colorbök); patterned paper (Doodlebug, KI Memories); Times New Roman font (Microsoft)

⟦Eclectic⟧

Gushing Geysers
Betsy Veldman
Rock Valley, Iowa

Supplies: Cardstock, rub-on stitches and words (Die Cuts With A View); letter stickers, patterned paper (BasicGrey, Die Cuts With A View); tag (NRN Designs); paperclips (Target); twill (unknown)

We took the afternoon off to play for Julia's birthday. She planned the whole afternoon....the Sioux Center park and then swimming at the Sioux Center pool, followed by pizza. You had a GREAT time at the outdoor part of the pool. We usually only come here in the winter when our pool is closed, so you had so much fun checking everything out. These water geysers were so fun. The big one in the middle is a circle you can stand in. You had a blast seeing how long you could stand in the center of it! Your sister on the other hand wouldn't go near the things. She hates to have water sprayed in her face, so she thought you were just sooo brave. You were her hero once again! August 11, 2006

Old World Charm

Ex-Votos of Saint Roch Cemetery
Madeline Fox
River Ridge, Louisiana

Supplies: Patterned paper, chipboard circle (BasicGrey); chipboard letters (Arctic Frog, BasicGrey, Heidi Swapp, Making Memories); die-cut letters (QuicKutz); chipboard frame (Daisy D's); acrylic paint, foam stamp (Making Memories); paper flowers (Prima); brads; copper accent (Nunn Design); ribbon (unknown); dye ink (Ranger); sandpaper

Hip and Trendy

B-ball Baby
Alexis Hardy
Franklin Square, New York

Supplies: Cardstock (Bazzill); patterned paper (Daisy D's, Hambly); chipboard letters, journaling tag, rub-on accents (Heidi Swapp); letter stickers (American Crafts); ribbon (Michaels); buttons (Autumn Leaves); chipboard accents (Creative Imaginations, Deluxe Designs); pen

Hip and Trendy

Princess
Becky Heisler
Waupaca, Wisconsin

Supplies: Buttons, cardstock (Bazzill); patterned paper, chipboard accent and letters, rub-on letters (Scenic Route); adhesive foam; sandpaper; pen

Graphic

So Loved By You
Liana Suwandi
Wylie, Texas

Supplies: Cardstock, heart shapes, patterned paper (KI Memories); rub-on accents (Creative Imaginations, Die Cuts With A View, Making Memories); sticker accents (7 Gypsies, Autumn Leaves, Making Memories, Provo Craft); brad (Bazzill); ribbon (Offray); ribbon slide (Junkitz); date stamp; adhesive foam; thread

⟦Clean Lines⟧

Dinosaurs
Nikki Merson
Troy, Missouri

Supplies: Cardstock; patterned paper (Arctic Frog); pen; Century Schoolbook font (Microsoft); Important Notice font (Two Peas in a Bucket)

9 upstairs
7 downstairs
2 in the car
1 at the dentist's office
(oops)
2 in your bed
1 in my bed
1 in the shower

DIN OSA URS

it's all you think about
morning 'til night
every moment,
eating, sleeping
breathing...dinosaurs.

Stan and you have a very interesting relationship. One minute, the two of you are chasing each other around the park, the next minute you're hitting each other mercilessly and one of you ends up in tears. You both love rough housing, but neither one of you is particularly good at gauging when to stop. Luca, you care alot about Stan and your feelings get hurt when he doesn't want to play the same games as you do. He's just a little bit older than you, and my bet is that has something to do with it. That said, you often ask when you're going to see Stan again, and usually end up having a great time goofing around. The two of you look like twins with your ultra-blonde hair, and people often mistake you for brothers. One day, Stan will return to England, but for now, I am glad you to can rumble through the challenges of boyhood together. (08/2006)

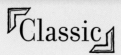

⟦IT'S A BOY THING⟧

⟦Classic⟧

It's A Boy Thing
Hillary Heidelberg
New York, New York

Supplies: Cardstock (Bazzill); chipboard accents, patterned papers (Imagination Project); die-cut letters (QuicKutz); rub-on accents (7 Gypsies, Autumn Leaves, Doodlebug); corner rounder; pen; Artistamp Medium, Blue Highway, Good Girl fonts (Internet download)

Graphic

Birthday Paparazzi
Wendy Inman
Virginia Beach, Virginia

Supplies: Iridescent cardstock (Paper Cellar); patterned paper (A2Z Essentials); chipboard letters (Heidi Swapp); rhinestone brad (SEI); rub-on star (Polar Bear Press); ribbon (unknown); pen

Clean Lines

Comfort
Mindy Bush
Ammon, Idaho

Supplies: Cardstock (WorldWin); patterned paper (American Crafts, BasicGrey); corner rounder; Pottery Barn font (Internet download)

GREATEST

our gift

SERVE OTHERS BE KIND
CREATE LAUGH OUT LOUD REACH OUT
ETERNITY JOYFUL HARD TIMES STRENGTH BLESS...

AN ORDINARY LIFE REMEMBERED
WELL BECOMES EXCEPTIONAL
... SO REMEMBER YOUR LIFE IN
DETAIL AND LEAVE
NO PART UNTOLD

『Journalistic』

Our Gift
Kay Rogers
Midland, Missouri

Supplies: Cardstock; patterned paper,
chipboard letters (Scenic Route); brads;
sticker accents (7 Gypsies); transparency

GREATEST

our

SERVE OTHERS BE KIND
CREATE LAUGH OUT LOUD REACH OUT
ETERNITY JOYFUL HARD TIMES STRENGTH BLESSING GRATEFUL SMILE

Imagine the day. It's the week before Thanksgiving (irony?), and I'm at school, sitting in the computer lab. My classroom was used by another teacher during my C&P, and I hung in the lab while waiting for my next class. Suddenly the OTP came into the computer lab. "Kay, we've been looking for you. There was an emergency call from Sanford El. You need to call them right away. And if you need a sub, let me know." Can you imagine the fear in my heart? Here were my thoughts. My brother and other sister were taking my dad to Ann Arbor, for a second opinion on a health issue. Something MUST have happened with dad, and they called Beth and she is calling me to tell me something is wrong.

I dialed the phone, calling Beth, to find out what was wrong. Imagine my surprise when the OTP informed me that Beth had been taken to the hospital, that she had collapsed at school. I didn't even know what to say. I'm sure I blathered on for a bit, casting around in my shocked mind, what do I even ask? Finally it came to me. "Was Beth conscious when she was taken to ER?" Answer . . . no. "So it's really bad?" Answer . . . yes. I almost collapsed myself. Problem was, to leave school I needed to leave lesson plans for the last two hours of the day. And call the rest of the family who was on their way home from a medical appointment, which I knew was stressful enough.

So I called the office to say yes, I needed to leave, and I needed a sub. When I was about to hang up, the OTP stopped me and said, you have another call. From your nephew. Now this is Beth's only child. Who is a deputy two hours away from our town. I can't even describe the depth of the relationship between Beth and her son. Words don't quite cover it. He was driving, much too fast I might add, back home to be with his mom. Some resourceful staff member at Beth's school called his police department, and convinced them to give personal information (phone number) so he could be informed of the emergency. Now I love this nephew. He is like my son. So the impact? No words for it.

So now I had to get out of school to the hospital. I was basically hyperventilating. Not pretty. Panic? Yep. Wrote a quick lesson plan, and Bill drove me to the ER. It was a blur. I remember seeing Deb, Beth's best friend from school. And Charlie, her principal. Why was he looking so pale? And my nephew's dad. Beth's ex-husband and his wife. Surreal? You betcha. "So what is going on?" I remember asking. No one was saying much at all.

They sent in the chaplain to speak with us. He explained that she had a heart attack, and was in a coma. They needed to shock her 7 times to get her heart beating, and she was still unable to stabilize, not breathe on her own. Was her family all here? "No," I answered. "The rest of our family is on the way from Ann Arbor. Her son is driving (like a maniac) and should be here in an hour. Her husband is on the road in somewhere in the south." Immediately he said, "you need to get them all here ASAP." OMG. He visited about three more times. Meanwhile we were in contact with her husband and my family.

The rest of my family arrived, and one Dr. came in. What he said was a blur . . . "30% function left in her heart . . . quality of life . . . she's in a coma." Those were the lowpoints. And have I mentioned my sister? She is 12 years older than me. The other teacher in the family. My other mother and my best friend. Can I just say DEVASTATED? Words fail me yet again.

They moved her up to ICU. Once we made it into the waiting room her son arrived. Think agonizing pain. Multiply it by 1000. That's how I felt. Then the chaplain comes in again. We'd like you to move to another room to speak with the Drs. You'll be more comfortable there. Well, I know what THAT room is all about. We sat in that room when it was decided whether Bill's mom was taken off life support. So begins the long walk down that same hall. The one we traveled when Janet (Bill's mom) died.

Beth wasn't responding to pain. Not a good sign. Family came, family left. Every Dr. said the same thing. Get her husband here ASAP. He was in contact with us, his mother, and the ER non-stop. I can't even imagine what that drive was like! Sat in the waiting room all night. Family, friends, coworkers, Beth's former students, nonstop. All night long. And the story unfolded . . . She was at school, in between classes. She called her DH on her cellphone. Pressed send, and collapsed. Meanwhile, her principal was walking out of the office when a parent stopped in. Her student had forgotten their gym shoes. Charlie, the principal, volunteered to take them to Beth's classroom. When he arrived, she was collapsed on the floor. He performed CPR. 30+ years in education, CPR training, first time he ever used it. Add to that the head custodian in the building, volunteer fire/rescue was available, and responded right away. Plus the head mechanic for the school district was in the bus garage. He was the lead CPR instructor for the fire dept. He responded right away. And the small town where Beth works has only one EMT/Ambulance. Which just happened to be ready to respond, less than five minutes away.

And in the ICU, Beth started to wake up. Early prognosis? No speech, no motor skills left, no memory, NOT GOOD. What did she do? She woke up, and told us about a dream about a family relative, and described the setting perfectly. There goes THAT diagnosis. Every minute of every hour of every day, slowly she improved. She proved every single thing that we heard would happen to someone in her state WRONG. In three days she was moved to CCU, then to a neighboring hospital for a pacemaker/defibrilator within a week.

Off to physical therapy, and she was able to return to teaching to finish out her last year in education, her retirement having been planned well before this incident. CAN YOU BELIEVE IT? I can't. Still to this day, I am thankful. Less than a year later, and there is not a day that goes by that I don't thank God for our gift. Our Beth.

WRITTEN BY

AN ORDINARY LIFE REMEMBERED
WELL BECOMES EXCEPTIONAL
... SO REMEMBER YOUR LIFE IN
DETAIL AND LEAVE
NO PART UNTOLD

thank you. thank you for being there for me. thank you for caring, for your joy, for your peace. I love being with you in good times and bad... sharing our tears, smiles, laughter. i thank you for being you and encouraging me to be me. i pray that God will allow us many more blessed years together. growing together, learning together. i'm truly thankful that you shared with me the real meaning of always and forever. It means so much more, now! i love you.

Journalistic

Always
Andrea Wiebe
Westbank, British Columbia, Canada

Supplies: Cardstock (Bazzill); patterned paper, ribbon (KI Memories); flower stamps (Technique Tuesday); solvent ink (Tsukineko); embroidery floss; beads; cardboard; fabric (unknown); watercolor pencils (Lyra); notebook paper; pen

JULY 06

FRIENDSHIP

I am so thrilled that I was able to capture beautiful photos like these. They were taken on July 30, 2006, at Sandy Bottom Nature Park in Hampton, Va. We were there for a Girl Scout hike and picnic that the girls had to attend. It was hot and muggy that day, so we decided to take our own hike instead of baking in the sun. Angel had fun swimming in the waters of the Sandy Bottom Lake and the rest of us just had a good time enjoying the peaceful quiet of nature in this urban city we live in.

moments

we give dogs time we can spare, space we can spare, and love we can spare. And in return, dogs give us their all. It is by far the best deal man has ever made.

—m.Facklam

SHAbbY

Friendship
Mandy Koontz
Hampton, Virginia

Supplies: Digital paper (ScrapArtist); calendar paper (Digi Shoppe); embellishments (Holly McCaig); brushes (Toastsnatcher); tags (SweetShoppe); Cinquinta Mil Meticais font (Dafont); Pea Marcie font (Kevin and Amanda)

Eclectic

Pure Joy
Karen Helmka
Longview, Washington

Supplies: Cardstock (Bazzill); letter stickers, patterned paper, rub-on flowers and letters (Three Bugs in a Rug); rhinestones, silk flower (Heidi Swapp); paper flowers (Prima); tag (Making Memories); brad; pen

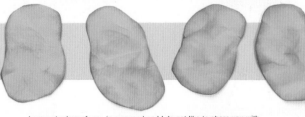

POTATO CHIPS

Potato chips. I just love you. I won't lie about it, you are food for my soul, truly. I have been eating you since I was a little girl. Since then I have eaten almost every flavour there is of you. Natural or cheese and onions you are my favourites. I also eat you with lots of dip sauce.....yum!

I can eat a bag of you in a second and I do not like to share you with anyone else. It is MY bag, you are MY chips. Because of you I need to loose some weight. So, I am buying the light version of you now, but I don't think it is healthy at all when you still eat the whole sack at once. Why do you have to taste so good!?

Clean Lines

Potato Chips
Corinne Delis
Alkmaar, Netherlands

Supplies: Cardstock (Bazzill); patterned paper, corner accent, rubber letters (Scrapworks); letter stickers (7 Gypsies); pigment ink (Clearsnap); thread; Arial font (Microsoft)

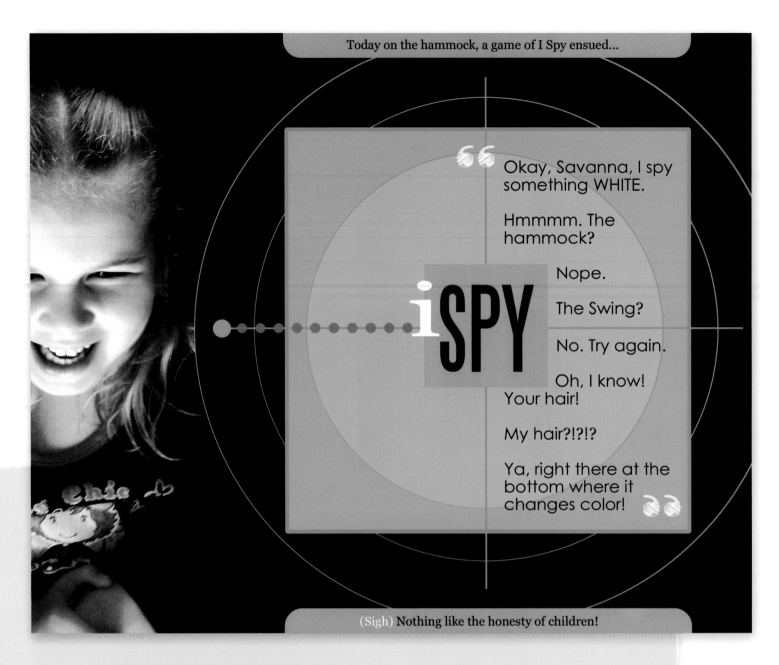

Today on the hammock, a game of I Spy ensued...

iSPY

"Okay, Savanna, I spy something WHITE.

Hmmmm. The hammock?

Nope.

The Swing?

No. Try again.

Oh, I know! Your hair!

My hair?!?!?

Ya, right there at the bottom where it changes color!"

(Sigh) Nothing like the honesty of children!

 **I Spy**
Deena Wuest
Goessel, Kansas

Supplies: Digital brushes, dots, paper, rub-ons, stamps (Designer Digitals); Century Gothic, Georgia fonts (Microsoft); Steelfish font (Internet download)

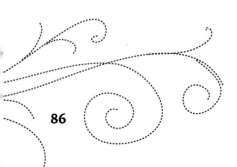

This is not an ordinary man.

Under that silly hat and that grey head of hair
lies a diehard competitor.
And softball is his best sport.
It does not matter that he is 65 years old.
He can belt a ball over the left-fielder's head.
He can drive it down the first base line.

Whatever you're expecting, don't.
He will always surprise you.

And don't say I didn't warn you.

Eclectic

Warning: No Limits
Tracey Wilder
Perrysburg, Ohio

Supplies: Cardstock; chipboard letters and frame,
patterned paper, rub-on letters (Scenic Route);
rhinestones (Westrim); sandpaper; staples; pen

my boys - silly as can be

They yelled for me to come to the den
and when I got there, they were proud to
show me that they had covered
themselves with underwear.

Each boy was wearing a huge grin
and they were giggling like crazy.

I asked them if they wanted me to take
a picture and I was shocked when they
begged for me to get the camera.

They posed for pictures, but they
wouldn't let me see their faces, no
matter how hard I pleaded.

After a few pictures, I put the camera
down but they continued to make
goofy faces and act as silly as ever so I
decided that a few more pictures were
necessary.

I have to say, life with my boys
is anything BUT boring.

Classic

Silly Boys
Ursala Page
Thomasville, Georgia

Supplies: Cardstock (Bazzill); chipboard letters (Heidi Swapp);
rub-on accents (Imagination Project); buttons (MOD); eyelets
(Making Memories); Decker font (Internet download)

Classic

You're Invited
Cara Vincens
Thionville, France

Supplies: Patterned paper, sticker accents (Flair Designs); chipboard letters, star accent (Heidi Swapp); brads; ribbon (Shoebox Trims); acrylic paint (Plaid); pen

Clean Lines

Ain't Nothing Bout You
Courtney Kelly
Colorado Springs, Colorado

Supplies: Cardstock; patterned paper (BasicGrey); letter stickers (American Crafts); brads; heart accent (Heidi Swapp); corner rounder; Century Gothic font (Microsoft)

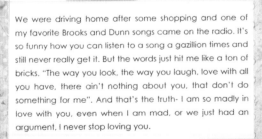

We were driving home after some shopping and one of my favorite Brooks and Dunn songs came on the radio. It's so funny how you can listen to a song a gazillion times and still never really get it. But the words just hit me like a ton of bricks. "The way you look, the way you laugh, love with all you have, there ain't nothing about you, that don't do something for me". And that's the truth- I am so madly in love with you, even when I am mad, or we just had an argument, I never stop loving you.

There **AIN'T** nothing bout you

that don't do something for me

What is it that makes life a fairytale? Is it relentless success and romance, followed by happily ever after? But how much is success worth to someone who has never experienced failure? Victory and success are recognized for their true value when they happen to someone who has had to work hard for them. And boy have we had to work hard! We have had our share of ups and downs, struggles and strife's, but we wouldn't change any of it! And yeah, sometimes we bicker and disagree, but you know what? It makes us that much stronger and more devoted to each other. We have to work hard to obtain each and every one of our goals. Sure, sometimes I wish things were a little easier for us, but a little hard work never hurt anyone! We have the things that are most important – health, happiness, and family! What we have is so much better than a *fairytale.*

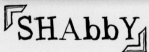

Better Than a Fairytale
Amy Farnsworth
Brighton, Colorado

Supplies: Patterned paper, buttons, die-cut accents, swirl accent, twill (Autumn Leaves); letter stickers (Making Memories, Scenic Route); chipboard flowers (Li'l Davis); paper flowers (Prima); brads; embroidery floss; ribbon (May Arts); bookplate (7 Gypsies); felt; paperclips; dye ink (Ranger); envelopes (unknown); Century Gothic font (Microsoft); Wedding Day font (Two Peas in a Bucket)

Eclectic

My Love of Green Apples Knows No Boundaries
Paola Lopez-Araiza Osante
Mexico City,
Federal District, Mexico

Supplies: Cardstock (Stampin' Up); patterned paper (Doodlebug, KI Memories); chipboard accents (BasicGrey); ribbon (May Arts); acrylic paint, brads (Making Memories); Antares, Arabella, Volkswagen fonts (Internet download)

SHABBY

Baby Brynley
Diana Dellos
Kansas City, Missouri

Supplies: Cardstock (Bazzill); chipboard letters, chipboard tags, index tabs, journaling tags, silk flower, transparent letters (Heidi Swapp); acrylic paint (Plaid); die-cut accents (Spellbinders); dye ink, glitter glue (Ranger); circle punch; dimensional adhesive (Judikins); sandpaper; string (unknown); pen; adhesive (Xyron)

please
mother
dear
I
love
you
SO MUCH
you're
the
best mom
ever
in the
whole
entire
world!!!

Confession #287
When I taught my kids to say please…I embellished it - a bit.
I hear this every single day. Go me!

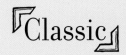
Classic

Please Mother Dear
Sharyn Tormanen
Howell, Michigan

Supplies: Cardstock; patterned paper (BasicGrey); acrylic
letters (Heidi Swapp); stamps (Technique Tuesday); chalk ink
(Tsukineko); pen; Arial Narrow font (Microsoft)

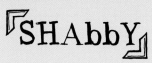

We
Tracey Odachowski
Newport News, Virginia

Supplies: Patterned paper (Autumn Leaves, Chatterbox); chipboard letters, flower (Heidi Swapp); rub-on accents and letters (Hambly); sandpaper; dye ink (Stampin' Up); pen

It is wonderful to see you both playing and getting along so well together, which may not always be the case at home, but it's a different story every time we go to the beach. You take turns hauling in water to mix with the sand to build a sandcastle or whatever shaped tools you have handy. Then you step back, giggle and admire your creation. Sometimes without any warning, a wave or two come crashing into it and send you both running and shrieking with delight.

together: 1. in the same place 2. in the same time 3. in company; unitealy

Eclectic

Sand Play
Grace Castillo
Anaheim, California

Supplies: Cardstock; patterned paper (BasicGrey); chipboard letters (Heidi Swapp); chipboard accents (Fancy Pants); letter stamps (Making Memories); dye ink; rub-on accent (K&Co.); ribbon, rickrack (unknown); pen

Sometimes when I look at the beautiful girl that you are, I marvel at the fact that you are our little girl, filling our days with laughter and joy. You amaze us with your intelligence and talents, and I realize that you could become anyone you want to.

While we waited for you I recall my impatience, watching the agency progress report on-line. I estimated the number of arriving children to waiting couples and surmised that the next group of children would have our little girl. When our phone never rang I was upset, and felt it was all unfair as I cried myself to sleep in disappointment. I had to trust in God, but it was not easy waiting for the Master Plan to come to pass...

I remember your arrival as vividly as it was yesterday... family and friends waiting with us at O'Hare International. Watching the screen for flight arrivals, pacing the floor of the international terminal, trying to catch a glimpse of the agency liaison inside customs, as we dutifully remained behind the ropes.

In a fleeting moment our wait was over. Jesse said, "there she is!", and on tip toes I could barely see the woman coming towards the doors. The doors opened, I started crying with joy. Kyle grinned from ear to ear. Loved ones gathered around, and one very elated father stooped down to take his precious daughter, Abigail Hope Lee, into his arms.

In an instant my dream faded... my daughter was here, in real life. Our first touch together may as well have been a pinch, I felt like I was dreaming. Through tears I reached out to hold you, my baby girl...it is a moment that will always remain etched in my memory.

As I look at you now, less than two years later, you are a reminder that prayers are answered, and dreams really do come true. Before you were born God knew that you would become our little girl. Every shed tear, every moment of disappointment, was a lesson to be learned ... all things happen in His time. As surreal as it may seem at times, I have no doubt of your very real presence as you hand me a Play-doh cookie, or share a cup of tea. You are mommy's little girl, you are a ...

Gift from **God** · *gift from God.*

Journalistic

Gift From God
Rita Shimniok
Cross Plains, Wisconsin

Supplies: Cardstock (Bazzill); patterned paper (Junkitz, MOD); flowers (Prima); brads (Lasting Impressions); ribbon (EK Success); cardstock tag (unknown); acrylic paint (Liquitex); pigment ink (Clearsnap); sandpaper; thread; pen; Palatino, Rendezvous fonts (Internet download)

93

⎡Journalistic⎤

The Gift
Wendy McKeehan
Batavia, Illinois

Supplies: Cardstock (Bazzill); patterned paper (Delish Designs); gold accents (Nunn Designs); brads; adhesive tape runner (Therm O Web); Amaze, Dauphin fonts (Internet download)

⎡Hip and Trendy⎤

Hide & Seek
Cari Fennell
Dewitt, New York

Supplies: Cardstock (Bazzill); chipboard accents, patterned paper, rub-on letters, twill (Scenic Route); buttons (Autumn Leaves); bookplate (Heidi Swapp); rhinestones; pigment ink

Sweet Baby
Lisa Tutman-Oglesby
Mundelein, Illinois

Supplies: Cardstock (Bazzill); patterned paper (Daisy D's); chipboard letter (Heidi Swapp); rubber stamps (Magenta, Paper Inspirations); flowers, word accents (My Mind's Eye); photo corner (unknown); cotton label (Me & My Big Ideas); acrylic paint, lace ribbon, safety pin (Making Memories); ribbon (BasicGrey, Jo-Ann Stores); button (SEI); rub-on accent (Cloud 9); dye ink (Ranger); corner rounder

『Anything Goes』

Go Fetch
Susan Stringfellow
Cypress, Texas

Supplies: Cardstock (Bazzill); patterned paper (Anna Griffin, Daisy D's); metal letters (American Crafts); decorative brads (Around the Block, Target); cat button (JBH Buttons); tabs (7 Gypsies); die-cut tags (QuicKutz); fibers (Bernat); flower punches (Carl, EK Success); chipboard flower (Pressed Petals); brads; circle cutter; embroidery thread; safety pins; pen

All For the Discount
Kim Shields
Spring Branch, Texas

Supplies: Cardstock (Bazzill, Paper Loft);
patterned paper (BasicGrey); chipboard tags,
pins, twill (unknown); brad (Rusty Pickle);
decorative scissors; image editing software
(Adobe); thread; Army, Dirty Ego, Earwig
Factory, PR8 Charade fonts (Dafont)

Farm Life
Alecia Grimm
Atlanta, Georgia

Supplies: Patterned paper
(BasicGrey, Die Cuts With A
View); rub-on letters (Polar
Bear Press); rub-on stitches
(Die Cuts With A View);
fabric flowers (Poppy Ink);
buttons (Autumn Leaves);
journaling tag (7 Gypsies);
dye ink (Ranger); square
punch; corner rounder; pen

Bowls
Amy Peterman
Muskegon, Michigan

Supplies: Patterned paper (Autumn Leaves, KI Memories); letter stickers (Chatterbox, EK Success); rub-on letters (KI Memories); die-cut chipboard shape (Imagination Project); velvet accent sticker (Making Memories); stamps (Little Black Dress, Technique Tuesday); dye ink (Stampin' Up); acrylic paint (Making Memories); pen

『Eclectic』

Happy – Fun – Play
Kitty Foster
Snellville, Georgia

Supplies: Cardstock; patterned paper, photo corner buttons, rub-on accents (Junkitz); pen; adhesive dots (Therm O Web)

❰Hip and Trendy❱

Mine
Melissa Kelley
Pueblo, Colorado

Supplies: Cardstock; patterned paper, puzzle
pieces, rub-on letters (Scrapworks); letter
stickers (Creative Imaginations); die-cut tag
(QuickKutz); paper piercer, round tag (Making
Memories); brads; heart (Heidi Swapp);
dye ink (Ranger); pen

❰Old World Charm❱

Treasure
Mary Russo
Westford, Massachusetts

Supplies: Cardstock (Bazzill); patterned paper
(Imaginisce, K&Co.); brass brads, rhinestone
flowers (Imaginisce); letter buttons (Junkitz);
quote sticker (Autumn Leaves); embroidery floss;
circle cutter; dye ink

I remember the days... When I got my driver's license in '93 all I needed was $10 to fill up the tank! And my little Mazda 323 hatchback could go for weeks on that. 13 years later I've still got an economical car but now I need $50 to fill up my Camry! I can still go for weeks on that tank but oh how times have changed!!

SIGNS OF THE TIMES

august 2006

[Anything Goes]

Signs of the Times
Gretchen McElveen
Helena, Arizona

Supplies: Patterned paper (KI Memories); letter stickers
(Heidi Swapp); notebook paper; duct tape; staples; pen

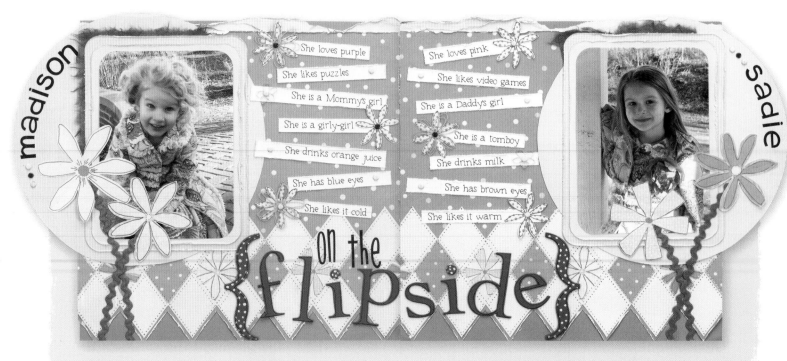

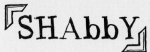

madison · · ·

· · · sadie

She loves purple
She likes puzzles
She is a Mommy's girl
She is a girly-girl
She drinks orange juice
She has blue eyes
She likes it cold

She loves pink
She likes video games
She is a Daddy's girl
She is a tomboy
She drinks milk
She has brown eyes
She likes it warm

on the {flipside}

SHAbbY

On the Flipside
Sandi Minchuk
Merrillville, Indiana

Supplies: Cardstock; patterned paper (Junkitz, Stampin' Up); chipboard letters (BasicGrey, Heidi Swapp); acrylic flowers, rub-on letters (Junkitz); brads; ribbon (May Arts); silhouette flowers (Heidi Swapp); acrylic paint; corner rounder; edge distresser; pen; Typeset font (Internet download)

don't ever forget me, grandpa

remember
Cruising
I CAN EXPLAIN

LUCKY

I'm so glad you're in my life.

Joshua and Dad were watching a movie with a character who had Alzheimer's disease, and both of them were getting teary-eyed. Dad commented that he already had a lot of parts failing, but not that. Joshua said, "I wouldn't like it if you forgot me. Don't you ever forget me—okay, Grandpa?"
"I won't, Josh," he said. "Don't you worry about that."

Photo 2004/Conversation 2006

GRAND TOTAL,

Journalistic

Don't Ever Forget Me, Grandpa
Debbie Hodge
Durham, New Hampshire

Supplies: Cardstock; patterned paper (7 Gypsies, American Traditional, Making Memories, Scenic Route); chipboard letters (Magistical Memories); letter stickers (EK Success, Li'l Davis); brads, buttons, word accents (American Traditional); canvas bookplate (7 Gypsies); circle sticker, index tab (Creative Imaginations); rub-on accents (Fancy Pants); acrylic paint (Plaid); thread; Roman Serif font (Internet download)

Old World Charm

Santas
Phillipa Campbell
Jerrabomberra, Australia

Supplies: Patterned paper (BasicGrey); stamps (Hero Arts); dye ink (Ranger); holly leaf cut-out (K&Co.); sticker accent (Pebbles); buttons, embroidery thread, fabric, fibers, tags (unknown); Kathleen font (Internet download)

Every year my Santa collection keeps on growing and growing. The Santa on the left is my latest addition. I'd been admiring him for ages but he was $125 and I didn't want to spend that much. But as luck would have it the Christmas shop had a closing down sale and I bought him for half price! The Santa on the right I purchased in Tasmania on our last holiday. He was another lovely Santa I just had to have. Photos December 04, Journaling June 05

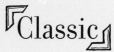

This is the Disney train steam engine. It goes all the way around the Magic Kingdom. We road on it 1 ½ times around the park before we decided to get off. Our conductor was hilarious. He sounded just like Adam Sandler as Bobby Boucher in *THE WATERBOY*. He said, "Momma said, to keep all the young 'uns on the inside because that is for their safety. And Momma said don't be smoking no cigarettes, smoking is the devil.". 4/22/06

Classic

All Aboard
Heather Carpenter
Baton Rouge, Louisiana

Supplies: Cardstock (Bazzill); patterned paper (Three Bugs in a Rug); plastic letters, ribbon (unknown); acrylic paint, foam stamp, rub-on letters (Making Memories); chipboard tag (BasicGrey); metal photo corners (Scrapworks); train stickers (EK Success); brads; folio closures (Colorbök); chalk ink (Clearsnap)

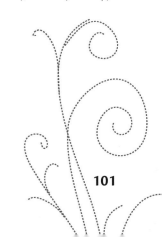

On Hindsight~ I remember when this photo was taken, choir farewell Where you are planted bloom party, at Mandarin Gardens. I was shy, gawky, nervous and pretty certain I was ugly. I had just permed my hair and was surprised that everyone thought I was pretty. At 17 years old, I wish I could have known then, what I know now, I'd tell this person that 1) It's important to have savings (2) Time is precious. Don't waste it. (3) Collect experiences, not things. (4) Don't wear your heart on your sleeve (5) Remember there's another side to every story (6) Everything has its time. Let nature take its course. (7) Stop buying so many things! Serious! (See point 3.) (8) Trust your instincts but don't just react to situations (9) Never do anything just to please someone else.(10) Accept yourself and don't worry about what other people think. (11) You're no fashionista. Don't even try it! Just be as simple as you want to be. (12) Try not to be anal about planning. Your life isn't going to turn out as you decided. But it might just be better than you dared to dream (13) You'll be fine. TRUST God. He has a plan for you. And don't forget to PRAY.

Photograph: 4 Dec. 1989.
Journaling: 12 Jul. 2006.

⌜Anything Goes⌝

Bloom Where You Are Planted
Lim Shor Wei
Coastarina, Singapore

Supplies: Cardstock (Bazzill); patterned paper (Making Memories); stamps (Blockheads, Pink Cat Studio, Plaid); letters (American Crafts); fabric flower stickers (SEI); pastels; water color pencils; dye and pigment ink (Plaid, Ranger); buttons, ribbon, rickrack (unknown); pen

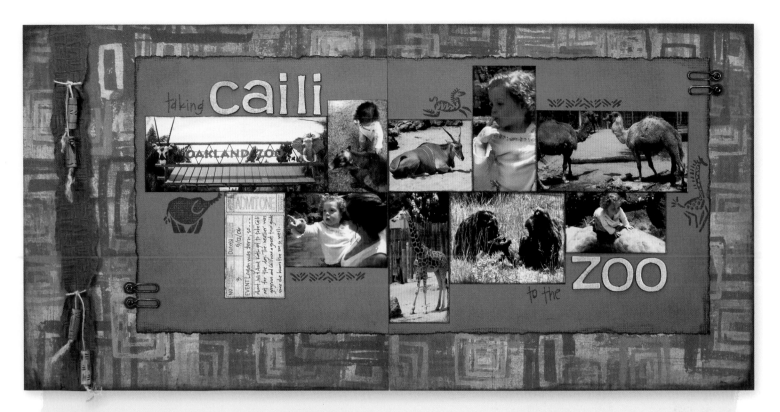

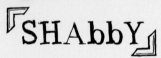

SHAbbY

Taking Caili to the Zoo
Kathleen Summers
Roseville, California

Supplies: Cardstock (Bazzill); patterned paper (BasicGrey); embossed cardstock (FiberMark); chipboard letters (Scenic Route); stamps (Sugarloaf); dye and pigment ink; (Ranger, Tsukineko); journaling card, photo turns (7 Gypsies); twine, wooden beads (unknown); pen

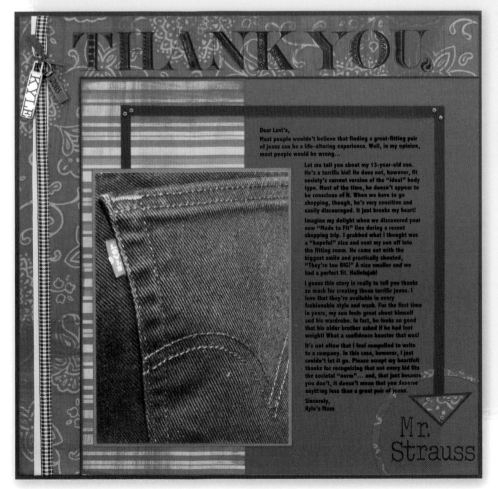

Clean Lines

Mr. Strauss
Kathe Cunningham
Buford, Georgia

Supplies: Cardstock (Bazzill); patterned paper (Junkitz); rub-on letters (7 Gypsies, Chatterbox, Making Memories); ribbon (May Arts); brads (Karen Foster); metal tags (BasicGrey, K&Co.); date stamp (Making Memories); circle cutter; solvent ink (Clearsnap, Tsukineko); transparency; adhesive dots (Therm O Web); Abadi MT Condensed font (Microsoft)

I wanted to take your photo because you were wearing my favorite shirt, the lighting was good, and the scenery at the Lake Shasta rest stop was ideal. To say you were cooperative is a stretch. This is the face you gave me.

Looking at this photo reminds me how much I love you. Because TRUE LOVE means posing for a photo (or 30) when you just want to eat breakfast...

True Love
May Flaum
Vacaville, California

Supplies: Patterned paper and transparency, rub-on accents (My Mind's Eye); chipboard letters (Heidi Swapp, K&Co., Scenic Route); buttons (Autumn Leaves); chipboard arrow (Technique Tuesday); pins, sticker accents (Heidi Grace); stamp (Art DeClassified); dye ink (Ranger); pen

『Journalistic』

2 Months
Cheryl Manz
Deerfield, Illinois

Supplies: Cardstock (WorldWin); patterned paper (American Crafts, SEI); letter stickers (Arctic Frog); flowers (Heidi Swapp); brads; stamp (De Creatie); solvent ink (Tsukineko); marker

2 months

2 months ago today I moved into your house to be your nanny. 2 months that have passed so quickly. 2 months in which we have learned so much about each other. 2 months that have made me so happy because of the little things I have come to love about you. Like the way you mispronounce your words. Or the way you say I love you a million times a day. Or the way you crawl into my arms to cuddle when I wake you from your nap. Or the way you giggle hysterically when I tease you. But mostly I just love YOU. Both of you. Unconditionally. Forever.
Y, Cheryl
Sept 8 2006

celebrating at Chuck E. Cheese's

『Clean Lines』

Five
Terri Davenport
Toledo, Ohio

Supplies: Digital letters (Designer Digitals); digital tape (Two Peas in a Bucket);
Avant Garde BK BT font (Internet download)

『SHAbbY』

Good Butt Jeans
Kitty Foster
Snellville, Georgia

Supplies: Cardstock (WorldWin);
patterned paper (Crate Paper);
chipboard letters (Maya Road); chalk ink
(Clearsnap); rhinestones; adhesive dots
(Therm O Web); Barn Door font (Two
Peas in a Bucket); SBC Love Mom font
(Internet download)

About the Artists

Karen Burniston is a freelance designer and instructor from Colorado. She spent three years designing scrapbooking products for Creative Imaginations and has also taught at scrapbooking events throughout the world. With a background in engineering, Karen's first style was very linear and geometric, but after several years her style became more eclectic and funky. She loves to mix patterned papers and embellishments and is definitely a "space-filler"! She follows a general rule to let the pictures be her guide when deciding just how funky, just how crowded, and just how eclectic she can be!

Mindy Bush is a wife, a scrapbooker, a photographer and a mother of six. She discovered her style several years after she started scrapbooking. Her style evolved as her photography got better and she wanted her photographs to take center stage. Now her scrapbooks are no longer about the latest technique or embellishment but about making her photos and memories shine.

Kelly Goree is a work-from-home designer and mom to three little boys who keep her constantly on the go. She's been scrapping for close to seven years now, ever since her oldest son was born. Kelly has considered herself eclectic in her tastes ever since she can remember. Even when it came to home decorating or being an art student in college, she could never quite commit to a particular design sense or style. So it came as a surprise that as an avid scrapbooker, she now has discovered her own style—one that is called "eclectic, " where anything goes. Imagine! Kelly loves all design and products and at some point in time, or even all at the same time, attempts to do it all.

Shannon Landen has been scrapbooking since 1995. She'll try any scrapbook technique at least once since you never know which one will stick with you! Shannon has been married to David for 17 years and together they have four great kids, a very hairy dog, and a cat who thinks she rules the universe and everyone in it.

Cheryl Manz is a 24-year-old nanny from Chicago, Illinois, and she loves all things colorful. Her greatest inspiration in life comes through words. She is the girl that always has a journal on her everywhere she goes to jot down things that people say, poems that come to her and anything else that inspires her throughout the day. Her proudest works of art are the ones where the words are the focus.

Old World Charm is the style **Helen McCain** flows most naturally to. She's always loved the details of old ancient architecture and stone masonry and the simple, carefree beauty of old cottages, the whitewashed, clean linen look coupled with romance. Although her personal style has fluctuated during the last couple of years from more modern to clean lines, and while she can learn and use elements from those styles, she always seem to go back to the incorporation of Old World, Shabby or Cottage. Helen lives in rural Wisconsin with her husband and two daughters but originally hails from Australia.

An avid scrapbooker for over six years, **Audrey Neal** discovered her style after taking part in The Dares, an online challenge site. By taking inspiration from a variety of pop culture sources such as advertising, fashion, and music, Audrey has been able to meld color and texture into a funky, playful look.

Kathleen Summers lives in northern California with her husband Ron and two children, Drew and Holly. Having always loved the aged and distressed look in art and decor, she naturally gravitated toward trying to get the Shabby look on her scrapbook pages when she started scrapbooking in late 2001. Kathleen hopes to encourage everyone to create scrapbook pages: "I used to be a CPA-firm accountant who didn't think she had a creative bone in her body... if I can do it, anyone can!"

Stephanie Vetne is a former attorney and writing professor who was introduced to scrapbooking in early 2004. Her style is classic and traditional and her focus is always on the photos and the stories they tell. To that end, most of her layouts have multiple photos and descriptive journaling. While she always enjoys playing with new ideas and experimenting with new products, her scrapping style remains traditional.

Deena Wuest started paper scrapping just after her daughter was born in 2000, and she reluctantly made the leap into digital in late 2005. Can you say, "love at first sight"? Once Deena got her first taste of digi, there was no looking back! Her style is clean, simple and graphic. If she looks at a layout she's working on and it reminds her of a magazine ad, she's happy! Deena always dreamed of being a graphic designer, but she considers her job as a stay-at-home mom as the absolute number-one priority. So when she found digital scrapbooking, her two loves merged!

Source Guide

The following companies manufacture products featured in this book. Please check your local retailers to find these materials, or go to a company's Web site for the latest product. In addition, we have made every attempt to properly credit the items mentioned in this book. We apologize to any company that we have listed incorrectly, and we would appreciate hearing from you.

3L Corporation
(800) 828-3130
www.scrapbook-adhesives.com

7 Gypsies
(877) 749-7797
www.sevengypsies.com

A2Z Essentials
(419) 663-2869
www.geta2z.com

Adobe Systems Incorporated
(800) 833-6687
www.adobe.com

Adorn It/Carolee's Creations
(435) 563-1100
www.adornit.com

All My Memories
(888) 553-1998
www.allmymemories.com

American Crafts
(801) 226-0747
www.americancrafts.com

American Traditional Designs
(800) 448-6656
www.americantraditional.com

Anna Griffin, Inc.
(888) 817-8170
www.annagriffin.com

Arctic Frog
(479) 636-3764
www.arcticfrog.com

Around The Block
(801) 593-1946
www.aroundtheblockproducts.com

Art Declassified
www.artdeclassified.com

Autumn Leaves
(800) 588-6707
www.autumnleaves.com

Avery Dennison Corporation
(800) 462-8379
www.avery.com

BasicGrey
(801) 544-1116
www.basicgrey.com

Bazzill Basics Paper
(480) 558-8557
www.bazzillbasics.com

Beacon Adhesives
(914) 699-3405
www.beaconcreates.com

Bernat
(888) 368-8401
www.bernat.com

Berwick Offray, LLC
(800) 344-5533
www.offray.com

Blockheads Paper Arts
www.blockheadstamps.com

Cactus Pink
(866) 798-2446
www.cactuspink.com

Canson, Inc.
(800) 628-9283
www.canson-us.com

CARL Mfg. USA, Inc.
(800) 257-4771
www.Carl-Products.com

Chatterbox, Inc.
(888) 416-6260
www.chatterboxinc.com

Cherry Arte
(212) 465-3495
www.cherryarte.com

Clearsnap, Inc.
(888) 448-4862
www.clearsnap.com

Cloud 9 Design
(866) 348-5661
www.cloud9design.biz

Colorbök, Inc.
(800) 366-4660
www.colorbok.com

Cosmo Cricket
(800) 852-8810
www.cosmocricket.com

Craf-T Products
www.craf-tproducts.com

Crafts, Etc. Ltd.
(800) 888-0321 x 1275
www.craftsetc.com

Crate Paper
(702) 966-0409
www.cratepaper.com

Creative Imaginations
(800) 942-6487
www.cigift.com

Dafont
www.dafont.com

Daisy D's Paper Company
(888) 601-8955
www.daisydspaper.com

De Creatie
www.de-creatie.nl/

Dèjá Views
(800) 243-8419
www.dejaviews.com

Delish Designs
(360) 897-1254
www.delishdesigns.com

Delta Technical Coatings, Inc.
(800) 423-4135
www.deltacrafts.com

Deluxe Designs
(480) 497-9005
www.deluxecuts.com

Designer Digitals
www.designerdigitals.com

Die Cuts With A View
(801) 224-6766
www.diecutswithaview.com

Digi Shoppe, The
www.thedigishoppe.com

DMC Corp.
(973) 589-0606
www.dmc-usa.com

Doodlebug Design Inc.
(877) 800-9190
www.doodlebug.ws

Dream Street Papers
(480) 275-9736
www.dreamstreetpapers.com

Dreamweaver Stencils
(909) 824-8343
www.dreamweaverstencils.com

Dress It Up
www.dressitup.com

EK Success, Ltd.
(800) 524-1349
www.eksuccess.com

Fancy Pants Designs, LLC
(801) 779-3212
www.fancypantsdesigns.com

FiberMark
(802) 257-0365
www.fibermark.com

Flair Designs
(888) 546-9990
www.flairdesignsinc.com

FontWerks
(604) 942-3105
www.fontwerks.com

Grafix
(800) 447-2349
www.grafixarts.com

Hambly Screen Prints
(408) 496-1100
www.hamblyscreenprints.com

Heidi Grace Designs, Inc.
(866) 348-5661
www.heidigrace.com

Heidi Swapp/Advantus Corporation
(904) 482-0092
www.heidiswapp.com

Hero Arts Rubber Stamps, Inc.
(800) 822-4376
www.heroarts.com

Holly McCaig Designs
www.hollymccaigdesigns.com

Imagination Project, Inc.
(888) 477-6532
www.imaginationproject.com

Imaginisce
(801) 908-8111
www.imaginisce.com

Jennifer Adams Donnelly
www.jenadamsdonnelly.typepad.com

JHB International
(303) 751-8100
www.buttons.com

Jo-Ann Stores
www.joann.com

Judikins
(310) 515-1115
www.judikins.com

Junkitz
(732) 792-1108
www.junkitz.com

K & Company
(888) 244-2083
www.kandcompany.com

Karen Foster Design
(801) 451-9779
www.karenfosterdesign.com

Kevin and Amanda
www.kevinandamanda.com

KI Memories
(972) 243-5595
www.kimemories.com

Klutz
(800) 737-4123
www.klutz.com

Krylon
(800) 457-9566
www.krylon.com

Lasting Impressions for Paper, Inc.
(800) 936-2677
www.lastingimpressions.com

Li'l Davis Designs
(480) 223-0080
www.lildavisdesigns.com

Liquitex Artist Materials
(888) 422-7954
www.liquitex.com

Little Black Dress Designs
(360) 897-8844
www.littleblackdressdesigns.com

Lyra USA, LLC
www.lyra.de

Magenta Rubber Stamps
(450) 922-5253
www.magentastyle.com

Magic Mesh
(651) 345-6374

Magistical Memories
(818) 842-1540
www.magisticalmemories.com

Making Memories
(801) 294-0430
www.makingmemories.com

Maya Road, LLC
(214) 488-3279
www.mayaroad.com

me & my BiG ideas
(949) 583-2065
www.meandmybigideas.com

Melissa Frances/Heart & Home, Inc.
(888) 616-6166
www.melissafrances.com

Michaels Arts & Crafts
(800) 642-4235
www.michaels.com

Microsoft Corporation
www.microsoft.com

MOD — My Own Design
(303) 641-8680
www.mod-myowndesign.com

Mrs. Grossman's Paper Company
(800) 429-4549
www.mrsgrossmans.com

Mustard Moon
(763) 493-5157
www.mustardmoon.com

My Mind's Eye, Inc.
(866) 989-0320
www.mymindseye.com

NRN Designs
(800) 421-6958
www.nrndesigns.com

Nunn Design
(800) 761-3557
www.nunndesign.com

Offray- see Berwick Offray, LLC

Paper Cella
www.papercellar.com

Paper House Productions
(800) 255-7316
www.paperhouseproductions.com

Paper Inspirations
(406) 756-9677
www.paperinspirations.com

Paper Loft, The
(801) 254-1961
www.paperloft.com

Paper Source
(888) 727-3711
www.paper-source.com

Paper Studio
(480) 557-5700
www.paperstudio.com

Paperchase
www.paperchase.co.uk

Paperwhite
(888) 236-7400
www.paperwhitememories.com

Pebbles Inc.
(801) 235-1520
www.pebblesinc.com

Pink Cat Studio
(519) 933-9375
www.pinkcatstudio.com

Plaid Enterprises, Inc.
(800) 842-4197
www.plaidonline.com

Polar Bear Press
(801) 451-7670
www.polarbearpress.com

Poppy Ink
www.poppyink.com

Pressed Petals
(800) 748-4656
www.pressedpetals.com

Prima Marketing, Inc.
(909) 627-5532
www.primamarketinginc.com

Provo Craft
(800) 937-7686
www.provocraft.com

QuicKutz, Inc.
(888) 702-1146
www.quickutz.com

Ranger Industries, Inc.
(800) 244-2211
www.rangerink.com

Rusty Pickle
(801) 746-1045
www.rustypickle.com

Scenic Route Paper Co.
(801) 225-5754
www.scenicroutepaper.com

ScrapArtist
(734) 717-7775
www.scrapartist.com

Scrapbook-Bytes
(607) 642-5391
www.scrapbook-bytes.com

Scrapbook.com
www.scrapbook.com

Scrapworks, LLC/As You Wish Products, LLC
(801) 363-1010
www.scrapworks.com

SEI, Inc.
(800) 333-3279
www.shopsei.com

Shoebox Trims
(303) 257-7578
www.shoeboxtrims.com

Sizzix
(877) 355-4766
www.sizzix.com

Spellbinders Paper Arts, LLC
(888) 547-0400
www.spellbinders.us

Stamped In Ink
(330) 241-3945
www.stampedinink.com

Stampin' Up!
(800) 782-6787
www.stampinup.com

Stampington & Company
(877) 782-6737
www.stampington.com

Stemma/Masterpiece Studios
www.masterpiecestudios.com

Strano Designs
(508) 454-4615
www.stranodesigns.com

Sugarloaf Products, Inc.
(770) 484-0722
www.sugarloafproducts.com

Sweet Shoppe Designs
www.sweetshoppedesigns.com

Sweetwater
(800) 359-3094
www.sweetwaterscrapbook.com

Target
www.target.com

Technique Tuesday, LLC
(503) 644-4073
www.techniquetuesday.com

Textured Trios - no source available

Therm O Web, Inc.
(800) 323-0799
www.thermoweb.com

Tidy Crafts
(800) 245-6752
www.tidycrafts.com

Toastsnatcher
www.toastsnatcher.com

Tsukineko, Inc.
(800) 769-6633
www.tsukineko.com

Two Peas in a Bucket
(888) 896-7327
www.twopeasinabucket.com

Urban Lily
www.urbanlily.com

Wal-Mart Stores, Inc.
www.walmart.com

WorldWin Papers
(888) 834-6455
www.worldwinpapers.com

Index

Find More inspiration in these other books from Memory Makers!

Ask the Masters!

Learn innovative techniques and solutions for creating flawless scrapbook pages from the Memory Makers Masters.

ISBN-13: 978-1-892127-88-4
ISBN-10: 1-892127-88-1
paperback
128 pages
Z0277

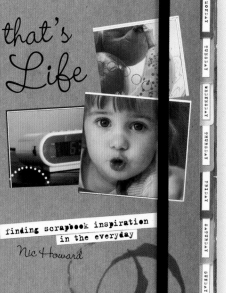

That's Life

Popular scrapbook designer Nic Howard shows how to identify, capture and chronicle everyday moments and daily routines in endearing scrapbook pages.

ISBN-13: 978-1-59963-001-4
ISBN-10: 1-59963-001-X
paperback
112 pages
Z0689

The Scrapbook Designer's Workbook

Join author Kari Hansen as she takes the fear out of understanding and using design principles to create fabulous scrapbook layouts.

ISBN-13: 978-1-892127-95-2
ISBN-10: 1-892127-95-4
hardcover with enclosed spiral
128 pages
Z0533

These books and other fine Memory Makers titles are available at your local craft or scrapbook store, bookstore or from online suppliers, including www.MemoryMakersMagazine.com.